Conservatism Revisited

PETER VIERECK

CONSERVATISM

REVISITED

Revised and Enlarged Edition
with the addition of

Book II: The New Conservatism—
What Went Wrong?

THE FREE PRESS, *New York*
COLLIER-MACMILLAN LIMITED, *London*

Collier-Macmillan Canada, Ltd., Toronto, Ontario

Library of Congress Catalog Card Number: 62-19968

FIRST FREE PRESS PAPERBACK EDITION 1965
by arrangement with the author

ACKNOWLEDGMENTS

During 1949, prior to the first publication of this book, the author published excerpts from *Conservatism Revisited* in the form of essays or articles in one or more issues of each of the following periodicals: *Harper's Magazine, Current History, American Quarterly, Forum, The Reporter.*

In 1962, prior to first publication of the Revised Edition, the author published excerpts from Book II in *The New Republic* and in the symposium *The Radical Right,* edited by Daniel Bell, New York, 1962.

Second printing March 1966

Dedicated to the memory of my brother, Corporal George S. Viereck, Jr., killed by Nazis as an American volunteer in the never-ending war for freedom.

Publisher's Note

ON SEPTEMBER 17, 1954, the Literary Supplement of the *Times* of London issued a special hundred-page number restricted entirely to modern American literature and philosophy, entitled "American Writing Today." Several hundred American writers were discussed. The two whose thought received the largest amount of space by far—a separate article of many columns on each—were Reinhold Niebuhr of Union Theological Seminary and Peter Viereck of Mt. Holyoke College. The article of the London *Times* on Viereck—ending "This is the hope that has come out of America"—is here reprinted because we deem it the most intelligent summary done so far of the ethics and political philosophy of Viereck's New Conservatism, a more perceptive summary than has ever appeared on this side of the Atlantic. However, even the best of summaries is no substitute for readers turning to the very first original document of the New Conservatism, Viereck's *Conservatism Revisited,* 1949. All other books of the "new conservatism" came later; and Viereck's new postscript to his 1962 edition (Book II, "The New Conservatism—What Went Wrong?") explains why in part this movement has deservedly failed.

New Conservatism in the Age of Anxiety*

MR. PETER VIERECK, poet and historian, can stake a claim to being the most controversial of the younger school of American authors. It is in his application of the enduring values of conservative philosophy that his philosophical and political writings (a skilful and adventurous skirmishing in the fields of political controversy and polemic, in which he emerges as the principal antagonist of extremists of the left and of the right) appear so pregnant with meaning and relevance for our tormented epoch. These values he defines as

> proportion and measure; self-expression through self-restraint; preservation through reform; humanism and classical balance; a fruitful nostalgia for the permanent behind the flux; and a fruitful obsession for unbroken historic continuity.[1]

Nothing could be more remote from a vital conservative philosophy—grounded in an abiding respect for history and a keen awareness of the faults as well as of the inherent moral attributes of humanity—than the strange blend of *laissez-faire* liberalism with religious confusion that so often passes for conservative philosophy in uninformed political circles, or the travesty of conservatism passed off as a genuine conservative philosophy by left-wing satirists. Such a philosophy is contained in the controversial work of William F. Buckley, *God and Man at Yale,* which anticipated his more recent writings in defence of Senator McCarthy. Against this book, which caused a considerable stir in American political circles, Viereck took an especially strong stand, in order to define his own position as a conservative thinker, and make clear what he himself meant by "new conservatism":

> Has a young St. Paul emerged from the Yale class of 1950 to bring us the long-awaited Good Tidings of a New

* Reprinted, by permission, from *The Times Literary Supplement* (Sept. 17, 1954).

Conservatism and Old Morality? The trumpets of national publicity imply it. But this Paul-in-a-Hurry skips the prerequisite of first being a rebel Saul. The difference between a shallow and profound conservatism is the difference between an easy, booster-ish yea-saying to the old order and a hard-won tragic yea-saying.

* * *

Conservatism is not a facile philosophy. It is far easier to dispense with law and dismiss traditional sanctions; to believe with a Robespierre or a Lenin that the violent overthrow of old abuses will bring a golden age. The conservative ironically wonders whether the golden age can be just round the corner; or whether, indeed, the greatest fallacy of historical thinking is to suppose the existence of a golden age at all. Revolutions like that of Cromwell (which turned into the military dictatorship that made Tories traditionally to fear and distrust an army in peace-time) or the revolution of 1789 do not support the supposition that all you have to do in order to achieve a better society is to sweep away the society that exists. The difference between the radical and the conservative is rather like the difference between Luther and Erasmus. Luther believed that the destruction of the religious order that prevailed would bring about the moral regeneration of Europe, and incidentally brought about the horror of the wars of the Schmalkaldic League and the emergent Germanism that devastated the remnants of the Holy Roman Empire in the Thirty Years War. Erasmus believed that the answer to the abuses of the existing order was to reform that order from within by enlightened criticism and inspired personal moral and intellectual example; and the effect of his life and teaching was the rise of the great humanist movement in letters that did so much to fuse classical humanism and Christian ethics in that unique and complex synthesis which we call the Renaissance of northern Europe.

* * *

The defence of our Greco-Roman-Hebrew-Christian inheritance the "new conservatism" would entrust to the intellectual. The betrayal of this precious heritage of spiritual values and moral example by what Sir Winston Churchill has so brilliantly called the "bloody-minded professors," whether of the Communist or Fascist variety, is the principal tragedy of our times. The confusion between the socially conscious, morally conscientious thinker, and the intellectual who assumes a spurious political character by climbing on to some popular political bandwagon, is fatally easy to make. It is also fatally misleading. To intellectuals the moral injunction, "by their works shall you know them," is particularly applicable. For "bloody-minded professors," who are ethically compromised by their toleration of political oppression, whether of a reactionary or radical complexion, are behind the "bloody-handed" dictatorships of our time. Instead of a political compromise between the intellectual, whose function is to be the ethical arbiter of society, and the politician, whose function is to put into practice those ethical values of which the intellectual is the guardian, there must come into being a free, honest and ethically enlightened demand, in intellectual circles, for moral integrity. The survival of intellectual, indeed of spiritual and ethical activity is dependent on a refusal to accept political slogans that are not tested by the touchstone of historic experience. What is wanted if society is to meet the totalitarian challenge of our time is not the appeal for an imaginary Utopia, which turns sour on the intellectual who recklessly demands it, but a healthy idealism which retains what is valid in tradition because rooted in fidelity to history and an acceptance of the effects of mature political experience:

> Here [says Mr. Viereck] is the real point: after twenty years of hackneyed liberal conformism in high places and of a cult of revolt-for-its-own-sake among writers and intellectuals, it is time to work out a more human view of humanity. And, by "human," I mean a view of society based on ethics and psychology, in contrast with an ethically-relativist and psychologically-superficial view of society based on economics.

This revival of ethics in politics Churchill demanded in vain when cynical politicians endeavoured between the two wars to forget that the only authentic peace is that which comes from the assertion of a standard that alone makes democracy tolerable and humane. Nor is democracy, if we mean by it no more than the extension of the franchise, necessarily a means to the achievement of an enlightened and humane society. Only when the people and their rulers are united by a common respect for law is it distinguishable from dictatorship. If democracy is not more than the rule of mass-man, morally compromised man, it is not distinguishable from "lynch law":

> The inner plebeian, the mass-man, is he who only obeys standards physically imposed upon him from without. . . . The inner plebeian is ruled only by his snout. And therefore the mass-man is totalitarian, tending towards a commu-nazi dictatorship of lynch-law.[2]

Against this mass brutalization, the conversion of the world into a global concentration camp, the free and creative thinkers of society will necessarily be in the vanguard:

> . . . all who are full-time servants of the Word. . . . This means educators in the broadest sense: philosophers, clergymen, artists, professors, poets, and also such undreamy and uncloudy professions as editors and the more serious interpreters of news. When they fulfil their civilizing function, intellectuals are the ethical Geiger counters of their society, the warning-signals of conscience. Their direct influence is almost non-existent. What of it? Indirectly and in the long run, their influence can be decisive.[3]

Above all, the struggle between the free mind and the compromised and totalitarian mind will be sustained by the perception that there is no freedom outside the law. Law exists expressly to preserve the freedom of the spirit, the moral activity of the enlightened intelligence. Above differences of emphasis on the degree in which social legislation is necessary to prevent the abuses of *laissez-faire* liberalism, the sovereignty of law remains as the defence of public as well as of private morality. The solution of the spiritual and moral crisis of western society, the achievement of a new moral and political creed, does not lie in comfortable and respectable conformism, but in a radical and triumphant refusal to compromise with evil.

*   *   *

The conversion of the class-structure of modern States into a society whose class-lines will be fluid necessitates the conversion of the principle of *noblesse oblige* from being the prerogative of a traditional landed aristocracy into being the foundation of a new pluralist society. As Mr. Viereck says:

> In this very exceptional, very American context, there is only one cure for the quantitative, anti-qualitative vulgarism that endangers all democracy. The cure is not to retreat into un-American class-lines in order to make some men aristocrats. The cure is to subordinate external coercion to internal self-discipline, in order to make all men aristocrats.[4]

How far, in a democracy, the balance between economic freedom and social legislation is to swing in either direction cannot be decided by rule-of-thumb, but only by reference to the ethical principles that forbid any accretion of governmental power, which thereby takes away the responsibility for social justice from the individual. The worst crime a government can commit against individual autonomy is, by the extension of governmental power, to encourage an unethical attitude of apathy among those whose position should render them responsible for the general good of the society. The responsibility of each in a free society is the only guarantee for the survival of all.

In nothing is Viereck's contribution to contemporary political philosophy of more value than in his assertion that the crime of a Fuchs, a Coplon, a Hiss, a Pontecorvo is fundamentally a crime against ethics, even more than a political offence. It is Viereck's assertion of the primacy of morals whether in politics or in art, that makes him particularly savage in his attack against moral relativists and the philistinism of "Gaylord Babbitt," the eternal faddist who is gullible to all the most superficial political *clichés* of the right and the left. The Philistines of to-day are no less pernicious because they conceal their intellectual vulgarity and moral obtuseness by a mask of cultural eclecticism. Viereck's condemnation of this lack of intellectual and moral consistency finds eloquent expression in the words: "We have seen the shambles caused by Munich deals with despots. We have seen the stupidity of shrewdness. We have seen the suicide inherent in narrow self-interest." To survive to-day requires far more than military preparedness; it requires that moral sensitivity which will perceive that the ultimate crime against spiritual as well as political liberty, in the context of the terror that the Fascists or Communists have created, is indifference. There is no redemption for modern man without a revival of the fundamentally tragic sense of catharsis, of universal commitment. Viereck's horror at this mass inhumanity breaks out eloquently in these words:

> When you hear eye-witness accounts of North Korean Reds throwing the American defenders of collective security into bonfires and burning them alive, when Communist leaders in Berlin smash the helpless body of the crippled democratic deputy Jeanette Wolff (crippled in a Nazi concentration camp) while shouting anti-semitic slogans at her because she favours civil liberties, and when you hear not one faint, subsonic peep of indignation against this from many who in America, England and France pose as champions of civil liberties, then to avoid emotions of counterhate does become difficult for our side of the barricades.

This quotation is given in full, because it accounts for that moral indignation which is so sizable a factor in accounting for what would appear at times the political intransigence of the Americans in such disputed issues as the recognition of Communist China and her admission into the United Nations. If Viereck shares this moral indignation with Americans, he also perceives how negative is an attitude of hate; it is not hate that is wanted in our rejection of Communism so much as understanding:

> Hate on our part would hurt us more than our enemies. Hate would trick our anti-Communist struggle into hysteri-

and agonized life dies not diminish the effect of his inspired continuation of Walt Whitman's ideal aim to fuse the material energy of man's inventiveness with the spiritual needs and aspirations that give to "spiritual democracy" its impetus and moral urgency. His poetry is all the more shining, as it brightly emerges from the distorted passage of his days. And it must be emphasized that the same aim animates the political philosophy and historical analysis of Viereck and the poetry of Crane. Harmony in an age of anarchy through the reconciliation of matter and spirit; will and energy. This is the hope that has come out of America—the hope of a "new conservatism" in the Age of Anxiety.

Notes

1. Viereck, *Conservatism Revisited*, 1949.
2. Viereck, *Shame and Glory of the Intellectuals*, Boston, Beacon Press, 1953 (out of print; copyright owned by the author).
3. *Ibid.*
4. *Ibid.*
5. *Ibid.*
6. The quotation and the Crane interpretation are from Viereck's monograph "The Poet in the Machine Age," first published in *Journal of the History of Ideas*, City College, New York, 1948, and reprinted in Viereck's *Strike Through the Mask: New Lyrical Poems*, New York, Charles Scribner's Sons, 1949 (out of print; copyright owned by the author).

Author's Note for the New Edition

BOOK I of the present volume is a virtually unchanged reprint of the book *Conservatism Revisited;* it appeared in 1949, not without controversy, as the first book of "the new conservatism" in post-war America. In the retrospect of 1962 here are its two most dreadful defects (both sins of omission):

FIRST DEFECT: the book's deliberate focus on Prince Metternich[1] (thereby picking defiantly the most unpopular rather than popular symbol of conservatism) was much too narrow a base for any well-rounded discussion of conservatism, especially in America. Metternich was chosen, among several other reasons of historical scholarship, in order to emphasize the point that international conservatism (Metternich era of 1815-48) and international liberalism (revolutions of the 1820's and 1848) should have joined hands against *Realpolitik* nationalism instead of fighting each other (fighting via Metternich's inexcusable Carlsbad decrees and other repressions and via liberalism's fatal self-identification with nationalism, especially the repressive anti-Slav nationalism of many German liberals of 1848). In not joining hands, both Metternich and the liberals made a mutually destructive error from which, so we then argued, modern conservatives and liberals must take warning. For in the context of World War II against fascism and in the related context of the post-war crisis with the communist version of totalitarianism, the book had aimed at uniting conservatives and liberals against both fascism (heir of Metternich's enemy: *Realpolitik* nationalism) and communism (heir of Metternich's enemy: Jacobin terrorist radicalism). Though this aim of conservative-liberal cooperation was and is a necessary aim, the fact remains that

[1] At the meeting of the American Historical Association, Chicago, December 1950, the author read a monograph defending his Metternich thesis and supplementing it with additional scholarly evidence. The monograph has been published in the April 1951 issue of *The Review of Politics,* University of Notre Dame, Notre Dam Indiana.

the focus on Metternich was too narrow. The remedy for this defect, for which there would be no space in the present volume of either edition, was to be a subsequent well-rounded survey of non-Metternich conservatives, American and European. And this the author did later attempt: in his book *Conservatism: From John Adams To Churchill* (Anvil paperback, Van Nostrand Co., Princeton, N. J., 1956); emphasis there is on Adams, the Federalists, Calhoun, Goethe, Nietzsche, Burckhardt, Irving Babbitt, Melville, Burke, Coleridge, Cardinal Newman, Churchill, Donoso-Cortés, Maistre, and Tocqueville.

SECOND DEFECT: While in no way endorsing the smug reactionary misuse of conservatism and indeed warning in advance against it at the end of the 1949 Foreword, the book failed nonetheless to foresee the appalling extent to which this misuse would triumph. Today the misuse exceeds the use in America. Today the new conservatism has at least half way degenerated into a façade for either plutocratic profiteering or fascist-style thought-control nationalism, that same fascist nationalism against which the book had proposed liberal-conservative unity. Indeed, as its front-page dedication to a fallen anti-Nazi soldier makes clear, the book's new conservatism was a direct product of the anti-fascist Resistance movements of World War II. As such, it was a companion volume to the author's war-time book on Nazi Germany, *Meta-politics* (New York, 1941; revised Capricorn paperback edition, G. P. Putnam's Sons, New York, 1961). These two books—these two themes—were to be thought of as inseparable: the first one fighting for the anti-fascist cause, the second one fighting for the *conservation* not of economic greed and privilege but of the value-heritage for which America rightly entered World War II.

In view of the genesis of *Conservatism Revisited* from a dedication to the anti-Nazi Resistance movements, the book may be seen as an attempt to perpetuate the ideals of these movements into post-war society by broadening and deepening these ideals. Broadening them: by including Stalinist and not only Hitlerite tyranny as part of the same totalitarian threat. Deepening them: by giving these ideals of liberty a

Churchillian traditionalist rootedness which a top-of-the-brain rationalist liberalism lacks—and for lack of which liberalism has often failed to withstand a Stalin, a Hitler, or even a mere McCarthy. The "new" kind of conservatism (as opposed to the stuffy reactionary kinds) was to remedy that liberal lack and thereby make freedom and a chastened liberalism more effective—more rooted—against thought-control tyranny.

Instead, the new conservatism is becoming the very opposite: it is becoming a façade for such attempted thought-control tyranny in America.

Book II of the present volume serves to repair this second defect of Book I by analyzing, along with what is valid in the *cultural* new conservatism, the ways in which the *political* new conservatism has become harmful to American traditions of freedom. Book II briefly examines that harm, both in the hands of a practical politician like Senator Goldwater and of a theoretician like Russell Kirk. Hence, the title of Book II: *The New Conservatism—What Went Wrong?*

Such commentators as the generally wise and balanced Clinton Rossiter (in *Conservatism In America,* revised second edition, 1962) have called ours an "eccentric and whimsical" sort of conservatism—after we broke with the majority of current self-styled American conservatives (pseudo-conservative radicals of the right, in our view) over these above issues of nationalist thought-control. The same pseudo-conservative rightists who discriminate against Negroes, despise the groping new governments of Asia and Africa, and stir up authoritarian nationalism against U.N. internationalism, these same thought-control rightists are also avowed disciples of Burke, their hero and the acknowledged founder of international conservatism. But Burke held a freedom-loving central position; he not only fought the leftist French Revolution but fought dictatorial George III on the right. Like those founders of Yankee conservative philosophy, the Adamses, Burke also fought against the Negro slave trade and against imperialist oppression of ˈIndia. In his famous warning against letting your neighbor's house catch fire, he defined and defended international cooperation against tyranny. (Not the rootless internationalism of Marxist radicalism but the rooted internationalism of a shared Christian-Judaic heritage of ethics.)

These facts perhaps tend to suggest that not the undersigned but the segregationist and thought-controlling rightists of America are the "eccentric and whimsical" deviators from the freedom-loving tradition of Edmund Burke.

PETER VIERECK

Mount Holyoke College
South Hadley, Mass.
June, 1962

Foreword to the First Edition: 1949

WHAT ARE THE VALUES we can live by in the post-war crisis?
To safeguard their peace and freedom, America and the
unconquered half of Europe are building a western union,
an Atlantic pact, a council of Europe. This may turn out to
be the most hopeful event in modern history since the catas-
trophe of nationalism, which shattered the traditional cultural
unity of the west. The western union is democracy's answer
to the conquering mission of Russian communism. America
rejects this mission, just as America rejected the still cruder
mission of Hitler and the fascists. Hereafter the material
strength of the west will not suffice without a unifying purpose
of our own, not class hate and race hate but ethic and reason.
The fate of mankind may depend on whether the moral, reasonable, rooted appeal of liberty can inspire as much unity as
the romantic, emotional, apocalyptic appeal of its enemies.

What justifies the western union and gives it moral cohe-
sion is the common desire to conserve a common heritage:
our free institutions. But vague complacent clichés about "our
way of life" are by now a glib evasion. Self-searching and
soul-searching are overdue.

A cynic "knows the price of everything and the value of
nothing."[1] These pages are a search; they are a groping for
"value." Their evidence suggests that cultural and political
conservatism may perhaps be the credo best adapted to sus-
tain a free and reasonable society. A credo not of some monolithic, systematized ideology but of a subtly linked pluralism
of rediscovered values.

"Conservative" (even Senator Taft prefers the word
"liberal") is among the most unpopular words in the American vocabulary. To be praised as conservative has become
an insuperable political handicap. This need not continue to
be so—provided that conservatives, often to blame for their
own dilemma, learn to conserve the humane and ethical
values of the west rather than the economic privileges of a

fraction of the west. I hope the reader will consider this conservative credo on its own merits and demerits. I hope he will not consider it on the basis of popular conditioned reflexes against a word that deserves to be scrubbed clean again, being the historic, traditional name for an outlook needed today.

The opening chapter attempts a definition and survey of conservatism in its cultural context of classicism and humanism. The two remaining chapters, based on a heterodox interpretation of Prince Metternich's political thought, examine respectively the conservative way to internationalism and the conservative way to freedom. In order to reassess the roots of our present western crisis, the historian must revisit the earlier crisis most resembling our own. This means revisiting that unacknowledged ancestor of our western union, Metternich's Concert of Europe, whose very defects can teach our own union what to avoid.

His union and our western union have at least one important goal in common: a cosmopolitan Europe united in peace. Then as now, the revolutionary enemies of peace were the nationalists: then Germany's middle-class nationalists, and now the "proletarian nationalists" (a newly-popular Soviet phrase) of an expanding Russian empire, whose original socialist internationalism has become one more tool of Russian nationalism.

Metternich's union and our western union have at least one important difference: ours rests on an incomparably broader popular base, being supported not only by the middle class everywhere but by the English and Scandinavian Labor Parties, the independent socialist parties of France and Italy, and the working-class millions of all non-Russian-controlled trade unions. This difference gives our democratic Concert its ethical justification and its chance of succeeding where Metternich's more aristocratic and monarchical Concert failed.

Metternich's misdeeds and misjudgments are here neither ignored nor condoned. A Janus-faced preceptor, he was conservatism at its shoddy and reactionary worst as well as its instructive best. The fact that he was both is a caution against oversimplifying him into all white or all black. Here the task is not to whitewash the black but to extract what is still valid from his political analyses.

There remains little to add about the important repressive aspect of the Austrian minister who guided Europe from the Congress of Vienna till the Revolution of 1848. This negative aspect has already been ably portrayed and rightly condemned by almost all historians of the period. Overlooked, yet likewise important, is the positive aspect of his Concert as a school to educate bellicose nationalists into peaceful, tolerant Europeans. How many of our widely known history texts ever mention his plan to reform and modernize the Hapsburg empire? His plan, as will be seen, envisaged a constitution, a parliament, and an assuagement of the nationalities problem through greater home rule. Such hopes were vetoed by the reactionary Hapsburg emperor.

In general, the police harrowings known as the Metternich system should properly be called the Emperor Francis system. Why is this not more widely recognized? Disagreement in high places was not carried on in public. Many documents about Metternich remained secret until the fall of the Hapsburgs facilitated publication at last.

The exciting new Metternichiana, including private letters and diaries of his contemporaries as well as state archives, are the basis of Srbik's big clumsy *Metternich* biography of 1,430 pages, published in 1925.[2] Using these sources, other scholars followed, such as the anti-Metternichian nationalist, Bibl.[3] These scattered fruits of research have yet to be fully assimilated by the historian; my aim has been interpretation of them rather than research beyond them. Although some of Metternich's eight volumes of memoirs do exist in English, there has never been an English translation of the rest,[4] nor of Srbik's two volumes, nor of all those newly opened archives on which he and the others drew in the 1920's. The American textbooks used most widely in colleges and high schools have not corrected their picture of Metternich as the reactionary bigot. Accordingly, his name evokes a hostile response in most of the American reading public—insofar as it evokes any response at all. This unbeloved conservative is the leitmotif of this book, not merely for his timeliness but also as a means to explore—yes, and rediscover—some timeless lessons of conservatism in general.

A definition of conservatism, in itself disputable, automatically arouses dispute as to the meaning of other political expressions. "Radicalism" will be used (admittedly arbitrarily, but consistently) to mean the violent, unparliamentary extremism of communists and fascists, which strikes at the "roots" of civilization. What about "liberalism"? No definition seems generally acceptable today, as shown by recent exchanges of letters in such diverse organs as *Partisan Review* and *The New York Herald Tribune*. One example of the confusion: 1949 liberals repudiate with a shudder, as somewhat to the right of Herbert Hoover, the bourgeois laissez-faire capitalism of Gladstone, founder of the Liberal Party.

None the less, "liberal" has certain enduring connotations that apply to both the Gladstonian liberal and the modern anticapitalist liberal. It connotes an optimistic secular religion of progress; sometimes, but not always, shallowly hedonistic; surely generous and sincere yet striking the conservative as often blind to the lessons of history. Frequently the real difference between liberal and conservative is in their reaction to such problems as: tempo of social change; need for tradition; confidence in modern technics; faith in the masses and in the natural goodness of man; feasibility of changing human nature; importance of utilitarian motives (economics vs. "ideas" in history); risk of extending full democratic privileges even to those engaged in forcibly destroying democracy; conflict between liberty and a leveling equality; absoluteness or relativeness of existing restraints and standards. These issues justify vigorous disagreement and debate. They do not justify hotheaded suicidal disunity at a time when parliamentary conservatives and parliamentary liberals must cooperate against an advancing and unappeasable police-state that would exterminate both.

Most liberals are not the fellow travelers of Joseph Stalin; most conservatives are not clamoring for a man on horseback. Red-baiting of liberals, or fascist-baiting of conservatives, was once a stupidity. In 1949 it is a crime. Mediation, reconciliation, and tolerant compromise are in better taste and in better self-interest for all groups working within the framework of civil liberties. Is it too much to expect that liberal conservatives and conservative liberals, approaching a similar position from different directions, can agree on some such viewpoint as Goethe's definition of the "genuine liberal"? "The genuine liberal," said Goethe in 1830, "tries to achieve as much good as he can with the available means to which he is limited; but he would not use fire and sword to annihilate the often inevitable wrongs. Making progress at a judicious pace, he strives to remove society's deficiencies gradually without at the same time destroying an equal amount of good by violent measures. In this ever imperfect world he contents himself with what is good until time and circumstances favor his attaining something better."[5]

Lest such an agreement lend undeserved comfort to the apologists of things smug and static, it must also include a warning to conservatives by the greatest of conservatives: "A state without the means of some change," wrote Edmund Burke, "is without the means of its conservation."[6]

PETER VIERECK
Department of History
Mount Holyoke College
July 14, 1949

Contents

BOOK I

Chapter 1

HERITAGE RENEWED:
THE
CONSERVATIVE PRINCIPLES

THE ENEMY WE COULD NOT BUY OR BREAK WAS THE ARIS-
TOCRATIC INDIVIDUALISM OF THE ORDINARY CITIZEN OF THE
WEST. IF ONLY WE HAD HANGED—AS HIMMLER WAS ALWAYS
ITCHING TO DO—ALL THOSE OUTDATED LEGALISTS, WITH THEIR
SQUAWKS ABOUT MORAL DIGNITY, THEN OUR MOVEMENT
WOULD HAVE SWEPT THE WORLD.

    —FROM AN INTERVIEW WITH A NAZI PRISONER OF WAR

IN OUR OPINION MORALITY IS ENTIRELY SUBORDINATE TO
THE INTERESTS OF CLASS WAR. EVERYTHING IS MORAL WHICH
IS NECESSARY FOR THE ANNIHILATION OF THE OLD EXPLOITING
SOCIAL ORDER . . .

    —LENIN'S ADDRESS TO A GROUP OF YOUNG COMMUNISTS

MY MEASURES WILL NOT BE SICKLIED OVER WITH LEGAL-
ISTIC DOUBTS. . . . HERE IS NOT JUSTICE THAT I HAVE TO
EXERCISE; HERE I HAVE ONLY TO ANNIHILATE.

    —GOERING'S ADDRESS TO THE GERMAN POLICE, 1934

   .   .   .   .

OUR CIVILIZATION WILL BREAK DOWN IF THE SCHOOL FAILS
TO TEACH THE INCOMING GENERATION THAT THERE ARE SOME
THINGS THAT ARE NOT DONE.

    —GAETANO SALVEMINI

all its citizens aristocrats. But not when it guillotines whoever is individual, superior, or just different.

In times of shallow prosperity, the conservative function is to insist on distinguishing value from price; wisdom from cleverness; happiness from hedonism; reverence from success-worship. In times of defeat, conservatism reminds us that we must still respect moral and social law, no matter how desperate our apparent crisis and no matter how radiant the ends that would "justify" our using lawless means. "There are things a man must not do to save a nation," said John O'Leary to Yeats in a discussion of nationalism.[7] Already in the fifth century before Christ, the historian Thucydides commented on the class struggle in Greece: "Men too often, in their revenge, set the example of doing away with those general laws to which all alike can look for salvation in adversity."[8]

The conservative lays the greatest possible stress on the necessity and sanctity of law. To him the "general laws," to which Thucydides referred, must be supreme over the particular ego of any individual or class or state. General ethics must restrict the particular means, regardless of ends. Let us suppose it were some day proved—as today alleged but unproved—that right and wrong are mere bourgeois prejudices of national or class interests and do not really exist. Instinctively we might say: so much the worse for right and wrong. Yet, even then, we should have to learn to say: so much the worse for existence. Sad experience would teach us that man can only maintain his existence through guiding it by the nonexistent: by the moral absolutes of the spirit. If this sounds paradoxical, it is of such paradoxes that human truth is made.

To rhapsodize over man's "natural, instinctive sense of justice," as opposed to established traditional legality, is a highbrow version of lynch law. Despite eloquent advocates of progressive education, the function of education is conservative: not to deify the child's "glorious self-expression" but to limit his instincts and behavior by unbreakable ethical habits. In his natural instincts, every modern baby is still born a caveman baby. What prevents today's baby from remaining a cave man is the conservative force of law and tradition, that slow accumulation of civilized habits separating us from the cave.

The accumulation is haphazard. As liberals correctly accuse, it includes much unfairness and much ignorance as well as good. When the bad is separable from the good, it is the conservative's as much as the liberal's duty to prune it. The dilemma on which liberals and conservatives split arises when the good and bad are inextricably interwoven by the centuries. He who irresponsibly incites revolutionary mob emotions against some minor abuse within a good tradition, may bring the whole house crashing down on his head and find himself back in the jungle—or its ethical equivalent, the police-state. You weaken the aura of all good laws every time you break a bad one—or every time you take a short cut around the "due process" of a good one. The lynching of the guilty is a subtler but no less deadly blow to civilization than the lynching of the innocent.

Conservatism belongs to society as a whole, for its purpose is to conserve the values needed by society as a whole. Conservatism is betrayed when it becomes the exclusive property of a single social or economic minority. This is the temptation every conservative faces, just as does every rebel on the other side of the fence. Many succumb. Many don't.

Sometimes the conservative orates too pompously about "maintaining established institutions." These can be discredited in two ways: by attack from the left or by exploitation from the right. When the conservative fails to save them from discredit, it may be the fault of the left. But it may also be his own fault for overemphasizing the attack from the left and underemphasizing the exploitation from the right.

Since the industrial revolution, conservatism is neither justifiable nor effective unless it has roots in the factories and trade unions. It was the Tories of the 1830's, like the seventh Earl of Shaftesbury, who fought for the factory laws to improve English working conditions. The laws were passed against the opposition of Whig industrialists and many Utilitarian liberals. And later Disraeli's Conservative Party, against the bourgeois opposition of Gladstone's laissez-faire Liberal Party, legalized and protected the long-persecuted trade unions and passed the workmen's social laws of the 1870's. This is why the English Liberal Party has now almost expired, leaving the Conservatives and Laborites as the new two-party system. When the urban industrial worker of England votes today—whether for

Folks and Art of Living, are tended by the serfs from whom he descended.

When he is the Sophisticate Abroad, who should know better, and when this results in a reactionary credo of class lines unhistorically restored, then the tour becomes a *tour de force*; intellectually-gymnastically, it does not come off; psychologically, it does not ring true. The conservative is by definition moderate in all things. He distinguishes between being conservative and being more royalist than the king, more classicist than the Greeks, and more pontifical than any infallible pontiff.

If humane social reforms seem "socialistic" or are against the fetish of laissez faire economics, that is not a substantial moral objection. When did we ever have laissez faire, and why is any merely material and economic system more sacred than the moral duty of compassion for want? A more substantial objection does arise when the proposed reforms cross a line beyond which welfare laws are inflated into the welfare superstate. Let us name this line the Statist Line. It is the line of diminishing returns for humanitarianism. Beyond it, the increase in security is less than the loss in liberty. Here arises the problem of bigness, the great unsolved problem confronting thoughtful independent socialists today.

In England, France, Italy, Germany, and Scandinavia the democratic socialists (Laborites or Social Democrats) are fighting for civil liberties and for the west against Stalinist communism. They are America's allies as much as any right-wing opposition to communism and sometimes more so. To attack them, when they are risking their lives against Russian aggression, is the stupidest and wickedest thing American conservatives could do. Aid from the Marshall Plan must exclude only the murderers of liberty: the Stalinists and fascists. To exclude more than these two outlaws from civilization, or to put antisocialist blackmail-pressure on another self-governing democracy, would be an outrage making America hated and communism popular.

Our need to abstain from such antisocialist coercion abroad does not mean we must cease to debate freely the issue of socialism. Allies can disagree. We must ask ourselves—and hope that our Labor and Social Democrat allies will ask themselves—whether their own ideal of civil liberties is not endangered when the socialist welfare state, no matter how benign its motive, can regiment that most precious of all "oppressed and exploited minorities," the individual.

For over a century, English and continental conservatism, whether in Tory factory laws of the 1830's or papal *De Rerum Novarum*, has tended to put social justice before laissez faire. None of these groups was remotely radical (and their reforms were usually opposed by the middle-class liberals). Similarly the American conservative will have to stop regarding as madly radical the long-needed laws protecting labor. These are the sane ethical norms of any industrial milieu. In fact, American social reforms are usually more timidly moderate than what European conservatives introduced two generations ago. Instead, the conservative opposition in America and England can become indispensable as the watchdog of antistatism, who does accept and welcome reform but growls warningly as soon as any group of left or right gets too near the Statist Line.

To keep on the liberty rather than total-security side of this line, the conservative should insist that social laws be expanded not demagogically but where needed; always with two-party participation; and never regimenting more of society than the minimum essential for order and justice. The alternative is the all-controlling, all-meddling one-party bureaucracy in which, to recall Lord Acton, "absolute power corrupts absolutely."

Social reform is not the same as egalitarianism. While serving the former, the conservative resists the trend of a mass-production age to sacrifice *liberté* to *égalité*. The radical, trusting the "sound instincts" of the masses, pushes the scales still further towards *égalité*. The liberal, in order to avoid a painful choice, sometimes pretends the conflict does not exist. Yet the greatest of liberal thinkers, John Stuart Mill, warned his fellow liberals that the tyranny of kings and nobles may be replaced by the even more stifling tyranny of the mob if "the inevitable growth of social equality and of the government of public opinion should impose on mankind an oppressive yoke of uniformity." In his magnificent *Liberty* essay of 1859, he noted: "Those whose opinions go by the name of public opinion . . .

nothing but bubbles of bliss can be seen on the surface; give him *economic prosperity* such that he should have nothing else to do but sleep, eat cakes, and busy himself with the continuation of his species; and even then, out of sheer ingratitude, sheer spite, man would play you some nasty trick. He would even risk his cakes and would deliberately desire the most fatal rubbish, the most *uneconomical* absurdity, simply to introduce into all this positive good sense his final fantastic element . . . simply to prove to himself—as though that were necessary—that men are still men and not the keys of a piano. . . . The whole work of man really seems to consist in nothing but proving to himself every minute that he is a man and not a piano key.[13]

The popular mind is probably on the right track in associating a conservative outlook with religion. But "religion" is a house with many mansions, finding room not only for literal but for symbolic interpretations of church dogma. Metternich, for example, called himself an *"homme d'église,* a free and strict Catholic."[14] Whether you interpret this as hypocrisy depends on how you interpret his typical linkage of "strict" and "free." This rational, almost 18th-century mind was less concerned with the supernatural aspects of Catholicism than with its function as a political and cultural stabilizer, a universalizer to halt the disintegration into separate classes and nations. It is possible to be catholic without being Catholic.

What falls more deliciously on advanced ears than ridicule of religion? How emancipated it sounds to dismiss in a moment's epigram an institution of nineteen hundred years! Thereby you prove to the smart world that you are marching in the front ranks of progress. The march, unfortunately, is into that flood of pagan totalitarianism which has drowned the liberals of central and eastern Europe. Unintentionally they had undermined their own best protection: the dikes of religious ethics which guard both liberal and conservative democracy against amoral statism. It becomes a question of persuading the liberal not to commit suicide.

With his vigorous criticism of abuses and his quick articulate conscience, the liberal is indispensable. Thoughtful conservatives should welcome his opposition, for it saves society from stodginess. Unlike the fascists and communists, the liberal and conservative agree in doting on the golden eggs of individual liberty, though the former may prefer them soft-boiled and the latter cooked longer before opening. Dispute arises about the all too killable goose that lays the eggs. For the history-minded conservative, individual liberty derives less from political abstractions and economic tinkerings than from Christianity and its extension of the free Athenian ideal.

Accepting slavery as we accept the use of machines, the Athenian democracy was incomplete. More loving and universal, Christianity was founded on respect for the infinite preciousness of every single individual soul. This Christian respect is what inspires political democracy as well as economic justice and must therefore precede both. Inward moral reform of the individual, which economic determinists are perennially "exposing" as a reactionary trick to postpone progress, must precede or at least accompany the outward material reform of society.

However, some qualifying of these assertions is in order at a time of growing obscurantism. Christianity is not only being abused by its materialist enemies in a revolt against ethics. It is also being misused by its romanticist friends in a revolt against reason. Reason is only a feeble flicker in a Stygian universe. But instead of joining the stampede to abdicate it, the humanist labors patiently to extend its San Marino-like frontiers against the night. The fact that reason is so frail and vulnerable makes its stubborn persistence all the more heroic: a vindication of the spirit of man, whose freely inquiring intellect is perhaps the most exciting miracle of all. When the historian concludes that religion, with its brotherhood and its ethical sanctions, best sustains a free society, he is supporting religion as a humanist in the Erasmus tradition, not as a theologian.

Protestant, Catholic, or Jew: for the humanistic conservative these variations, whose differences should not be minimized, are yet within the same ethical and historical framework. Christianity is the needed time-capsule conserving and fusing the four ancestries of western man: the stern moral commandments and social justice of Judaism; the love for beauty and for untrammeled intellectual speculation of the free Hellenic mind; the Roman Empire's universalism and its exaltation of law; and the Aristotelianism, Thomism, and antinominalism included in the Middle Ages. These heritages are sometimes mutually conflicting. Society is ever fusing them in new proportions to meet the ever shifting emphasis on morality, beauty, intellect, legalism, or universality. To some degree all must be present. The razor's-edge tension of the delicate and vulnerable balance between them is perhaps what goads western man to greatness and gives him his creativity, his élan.

This Christian time-capsule of our four heritages is still the best school for taming barbarians. Nietzsche, the pious Antichrist, noted this with esthetic regret. Conservatives note it with relief, for they claim that every human being is by nature barbarous, capable of every insanity and atrocity. Unless the pruned and geometric gardens that Le Nôtre built at Versailles are superior to the chaotic jungles hailed by romanticism, unless art and artifice and classicism and formal social convention are preferable to nature and the cult of naturalness, the distinction between man and animal is an outworn snobbism. And indeed, since the 1930's, this trifling 10,000-year-old caprice of trying to differ from the beasts is being liquidated by the spread of Progress over one-fifth of the globe, from the mass graves of Maidanek to the slave kennels of Siberia. As Albert Guérard warned in 1939,

> The romantic rebellion against discipline, measure, and sanity, that is to say against civilization, [is] the chief problem in European culture—philosophy and art no less than politics—for the last 200 years; a problem too deep for any "economic interpretation." The disastrous surge of the elemental has been made possible only because the educated have betrayed civilization and exalted the abyss. "Better a tragic and magnificent Götterdämmerung than a thousand years of peace!" It is the apologists of dynamic chaos who have pushed the world back into chaos.[15]

Conservatism, which is for politics what classicism is for literature, is in turn the political secularization of the doctrine of original sin. In contrast, radicalism is Rousseau's "natural goodness of man" collectivized into a touching political faith in "the masses." Nazi radicalism equates Rousseau's Noble Savage with the racial mass (the *Volk*); Marxist radicalism equates him with the economic mass (the proletariat). But he is not worshipped like this by the churches. The churches, Protestant, Catholic, or the closely related Jewish, draw the fangs of the Noble Savage and clip his ignoble claws. By so doing, and when and if they practice what they preach, they are performing their share of the conservative function, the function of spanning the gap between the cave man and society. Marx gave the ablest summary of the issue when he dreaded religion as "the opiate of the people"—that is, the tamer, pacifier, civilizer of the people. The contemporary uncivilizers are only logical in persecuting religion.

An imperative of Christian ethics, a test of its sincerity, is to fight—without hedging or qualification—the pagan, unChristian obscenity of anti-Semitism. He who is against any human race, is against the whole human race. Discrimination against the civil liberties of any minority is the opening wedge against liberty itself. No wonder many German nationalists raged when the not-so-reactionary Congress of Vienna confirmed the emancipation of the Jews begun under the French. In fact, many of Metternich's nationalist foes after 1815 made hate against some rival nationality their most useful weapon against his internationalism.

The great taming process of civilization includes not only the past, not only the barbarian invasion from outside the west (the Germanic waves that beat down Rome, or the Tartars who ended the westernized Russia of Kiev). It must also include the internal invasion of today, the barbarian invasion from below: the mass-man. The terms "mass-man" and "barbarian" are not a snobbism invoked against the poor or the primitive. The mass-man, the underground barbarian of our urban jungles, does not necessarily lack wealth or brains or technics. As likely to be a banker as a bricklayer, the massman believes that the end justifies the means and says with Goebbels: "Important is not what is right but what wins."[16]

The issue is ethics, not technics. Mass-man means blindness. It means blindness to the standards of conduct which civilization has over eons gradually imposed upon human nature.

This process is artificial—in the best sense of the word. The mass-man's barbarism is natural. So is lynch law.

Education means not only the school but the home, the church, the public and private submission to ethics. In this sense, the increase in education has not kept up with the increase in population. After remaining fairly static for many centuries, the population of the western world suddenly tripled after the industrial revolution. This has been the hugest and fastest population increase in history. With ethics lagging behind both technics and births, and with material power outracing the spiritual power needed to control it, the urban age has spawned the numberless nomads of modernity.

A morally illiterate culture of unhappy and untragic pleasure-seekers has failed to root its masses in the universals of civilization. As we have seen, this is partly due to the radical Rousseauistic cult of naturalness, the cult of revolt and anti-artifice and antitradition. And it is partly due to the satanic pride in one's own unchecked ego, a pride based on deeming the ego naturally good and ignoring the problem of evil.

The result is Neanderthalers with a high I.Q.; giggling apes playing at snowball-fights with atom bombs; efficient barbarians applying to uncivilized ends the subtlest technical achievements of civilization. These problems are the subject of Ortega y Gasset's *The Revolt of the Masses:* "There is no culture where there are no standards to which our fellow-men can have recourse. There is no culture where there are no principles of legality to which to appeal. . . . Properly speaking, there are no barbarian standards. Barbarism is the absence of standards to which appeal can be made." Trying to systematize some of the contradictory visions of Nietzsche, Ortega observed in 1930:

> Under the species of Syndicalism and Fascism there appears for the first time in Europe a type of man who does not want to give reasons or to be right but simply shows himself resolved to impose his opinions. . . . Here I see the most palpable manifestation of the new mentality of the masses, due to their having decided to rule society without the capacity for doing so. . . . Hence, the "new thing" in

Europe is to "have done with discussions;" and detestation is expressed for all forms of intercommunion which imply acceptance of objective standards, ranging from conversation to Parliament, and taking in science. This means a renunciation of the common life based on culture, which is subject to standards, and a return to the common life of barbarism. All the normal processes are suppressed in order to arrive directly at the imposition of what is desired. . . .

Civilization is nothing else than the attempt to reduce force to being the last resort. . . . "Direct action" consists in inverting the order and proclaiming violence as the first resort, or strictly as the sole resort. It is the norm which proposes the annulment of all norms. . . . It is the Magna Charta of barbarism.[17]

Nietzsche was perhaps the first to diagnose the modern mass-man. He associated him with nationalism and with worship of quantity and power, as opposed to quality and thought. Warning against "atavistic attacks of patriotism and soil attachment," Nietzsche in 1886 wrote an indictment of the Bismarckian Europe of power and empire, an indictment even more valid for our own time: "It is the age of the masses: they lie on their belly before everything that is massive. And so also in politics. A statesman who rears up for them a new Tower of Babel, some monstrosity of empire and power, they call 'great'—what does it matter that we more prudent and *conservative* ones do not meanwhile give up the old belief that it is only the great thought that gives greatness to an action?"[18]

Yet Nietzsche's scorn of Christian ethics makes him at times the agent of this barbarism as well as its unmasker. A more reliable, if less exalted guide through the Stalin-Hitler inferno of mass-men and Führers is Nietzsche's colleague in Switzerland, the historian Burckhardt (1818-97):

"I have a premonition which sounds like utter folly, and yet it will not leave me: the military state will become one single vast factory. Those hordes of men in the great industrial centers cannot be left indefinitely to their greed and want. What must logically come is a definite and supervised stint of misery, with promotions and uniforms, daily begun and ended to the sound of drums. . . . In the delightful 20th century, authoritarianism will raise its head again, and a terrifying head it will be. . . . The big damage was done in the previous [18th] century, especially by Rousseau with his preaching of the goodness of human nature. . . . As any child can see, this resulted in the complete dissolution of the concept of [legitimate] authority in the heads of mortals, whereupon they periodically had to be subjected to naked [illegitimate] force instead. . . .

"My picture of the *terribles simplificateurs* who will overrun Europe, is no pleasant one . . . naked force in command and the silencing of opposition. . . . To get re-elected, the national leaders must win over the most turbulent segments of the masses. The latter demand that something be constantly happening; otherwise, they won't believe 'Progress' is marching on. . . . One after the other, a sacrifice must be made of social order, property, religion, distinguished codes of conduct, higher learning—so long as the masses can bring pressure on their leaders. . . . This power can only derive from evil, and its results will make your hair stand on end. . . . People no longer believe in principles but will probably periodically believe in saviors. . . . Long voluntary subjection under individual Fuehrers is in prospect."[19]

Writing to Tsar Alexander in 1820, Metternich blamed the world's lawlessness and terror on what he called "the presumptuous man." His description of the presumptuous man as "the sole judge of his own actions" anticipates Ortega's mass-man and Burckhardt's *terribles simplificateurs*. For the presumption as "the natural effect of the rapid progression of contributed to make them, and it would be beneath a man of his parts to recognize the limits traced by rude and ignorant generations. Power resides in himself." Metternich defines this presumptuous man, "laws have no value because he has not the human mind towards the perfecting of so many things. . . . The progress of the human mind has been extremely rapid in the last three centuries. This progress [has] been accelerated more rapidly than the growth of wisdom, the only counterpoise to passions and to error."[20] Metternich's contrast between the slow ripeness of wisdom and the fast "progress" of technics and of mere information is a fitting close to this contrast between the conservative and the mass-man.

From here the inquiry turns logically to the story of Metternich. It is equally the story of the German revolt against Europe. The theme is the last stand of western oneness— "cosmopolite" was Metternich's favorite adjective—against the mass-men of nationalism. And, on the other flank, against the mass-men of class-war radicalism. In our own day these two rival antiethical currents of the 19th century, both romantic nationalism and materialist radicalism, have been united in varying proportions by German "national socialism" and by Russian national bolshevism.

Last year was the centennial of the anticonservative revolution of 1848. Metternich, whom it overthrew, once said: "In a hundred years the historian will understand me better."[21] Now the hundred years have passed. When a statesman has lived at the turning-point of a period of transition, his historical position becomes paradoxical. The new order sees as negative and reactionary those very policies which seemed positive and educational to the old order. When, however, both orders have passed away with both their viewpoints, such a statesman is due for re-examination. An unprejudiced return to the sources is then called for.

Such a moment in history has arrived for Clemens Metternich. In the expanse he once dominated—central and eastern Europe and the Italian peninsula,—his world and that of his liberal opponents have both been destroyed by the Nazi conflagration. Both have become history rather than current events and can now be sized up in a new light. After the other conflagration, that of the Napoleonic wars, Metternich's program for his demoralized and convalescent Europe was repose and re-education. The feverish patients in what he called the "world hospital" were to be educated in the principles of internationalism, conservatism, and peace. Against odds, he hoped thereby to achieve "the rebirth of Europe," "the new era of salvation."[22] His principles achieved some striking failures and some striking successes and in both cases gave their imprint to Europe for half a century.

2

"WHAT will our friend Metternich say of this great triumph?" asked Nesselrode, the Russian Foreign Minister. He was commenting on the victory of Navarino Bay, 1827, where the Turks were defeated by a treacherous surprise attack, and he answered his own question as follows:

"He will repeat his old, tiresome principles; he will talk of right;—*vive la force!* It is might which rules the world nowadays, and I am very glad to find that I and my comrades can leave the regulating of affairs to admirals. These are the men to cut the matter short! Never has there been glory comparable to this moment!"

For one who sees Hitlerism as the logical result of such *Realpolitik*, Metternich reaches his greatest stature in his calm comment on Nesselrode's gloating. "This," said Metternich, "is how Carnot and Danton, and afterwards their imitators, thought and spoke. They were signally overthrown, however, by the same old and tiresome principles."[1]

These two conflicting quotations remind us that the age of Metternich was, among other things, a conflict between two codes of international ethics: "force" and "principles." After 1848, and still more after 1870, "force" was to triumph over "principles" because of the triumph of nationalism, which replaced the oneness of western civilization with the patriotic Balkanizing of Europe. The principles Metternich claimed for his conservative internationalism are suggested by *"Kraft im Recht,"* the motto he chose for his coat of arms.[2] Literally it means "Strength in Law." There is perhaps the further, more figurative implication of "Force within Law," a meaning in accord with the philosophy expressed in his "Political Testament." The difference between a world of unchecked national

55

sovereignty and a United Nations world is the difference of outlook between *"Vive la force"* and *"Kraft im Recht."*

"Not by speeches and majority votes are the great questions of the day decided . . . but by blood and iron":—this phrase of Bismarck's in 1863 reflects a political universe incompatible with that reflected by Metternich's remark at the Congress of Laibach: "Is there anything in the world today which can take the place of ink, pens, a *conference table* with its green cover, and a few greater or smaller bunglers?"[3] Metternich's aristocratic system depended on diplomacy. Democratic liberalism depended on what Bismarck dismissed as "majority votes." Both systems preferred "speeches" to "blood." Both sought to internationalize Europe. Both failed because of the civil war between them. The men who believed in discussion, both the democrats and the aristocratic diplomats, were replaced by the men of action, who turned Europe's common heritage into chaos.

The battle between right and right is more tragic than the battle between right and wrong. Both Metternich and the liberals of 1848 were right or at least shared half-truths, for both sought a peaceful and ethical and cosmopolitan Europe. They should have joined their respective half-truths against the whole-lies of their real enemies: the self-styled realists of antiethical *Realpolitik*, the racists, the militarists, the war-planning Irredentists. Because the liberals and conservatives never joined their halves, these nationalist forebears of fascism could triumph, just as a similar disunity invites fascism and communism today. Since 1815 or even since 1789, middle-class internationalism and monarchico-aristocratic internationalism spent their energies in successfully undermining each other's claims on Europe's loyalty. Wounding each other fatally in 1848, they created a vacuum of loyalty which nationalism filled as *tertius gaudens*.

Many liberals combined internationalism with a liberal idealized version of nationalism, such as Herder preached. The hope that nationalism would turn out liberal, is the error that destroyed liberalism and democracy in central Europe. It made German liberals back the nationalists against Metternich's relatively mild repressions in 1848 and then, for the sake of

German unity, sell out their liberalism after 1866 to Prussian militarism. Even in the west, the liberals who dreaded nationalism (Mill called it "the new barbarism") were outnumbered by the liberals—Mazzini, Gladstone, Wilson—who deemed a liberal nationalism feasible. In a Europe of overlapping nationalities, a Europe of endless Alsace-Lorraines, Schleswig-Holsteins, Sudetenlands, Polish Corridors, Transylvanias, Bessarabias, Macedonias, Trentinos, and Triestes—in such a jigsaw-puzzle Europe, nationalism could in no case have asserted its claims except by unliberal blood-and-iron methods. Right from the start, this inner contradiction doomed liberal hopes for a peaceful nationalism, even if there had never been the antinationalist Metternichian opposition, on which Europe's failure to develop a liberal nationalism is often blamed today.

Once upon a time there really was a period when "the great questions of the time" were generally decided by "speeches" instead of "blood and iron," at "conference tables with green covers" instead of on battlefields. During this era Europe enjoyed what is perhaps the longest peace since the Roman peace of the five Good Emperors, which had ended when Marcus Aurelius died at Vienna (Vindobona) in the year 180. To be sure, Navarino Bay and the dispute over Greece were an almost fatal challenge; but this danger passed again without any war between the signatories of 1815, none until the tragic Crimean War of 1854—for that matter, no lengthy wars nor widespread general wars between 1815 and 1914.

The nearest modern equivalent of Rome's long, prosperous, creative peace was the "Metternich era," a phrase with horrific connotations for many readers. Politically, the peace created by the Congress of Vienna was based on conservatism, in which the psychological pressure of tradition and the material pressure of the rural classes (aristocracy and peasantry) restrained but did not stifle the growing urban middle classes of central Europe. Philosophically, the peace was based on Metternich's monotonously reiterated principle that "the cultivation of the ego must recognize bounds in the lives of states as in private life, in order not to be reduced to absurdity."[4]

According to the opposite type of statesmanship, it is absurd to bound at all what Salandra called the nation's *sacro egoismo*. The successful Hitler aggressions of the 1930's and the successful Stalin aggressions of the 1940's, both symbolized by the resignation of President Benes in 1938 and 1948, prove that a League of Nations or a United Nations cannot keep peace without the power to enforce it. Metternich's Concert of Europe did have such power. And it did keep the peace.

More than a century before the founding of the U. N., Metternich viewed his continent not as separate clashing races and nations but as a single indivisible nation, "the Republic of Europe." Here is how his friend Gentz expressed the great truth that was also Metternich's basic assumption:

> Through their geographic position, through the uniformity of their customs, their laws, their needs, their way of life, and their culture, all the states of this continent form a great political league, which with some justification has been dubbed the *European Republic*. . . . The various members of this *League of Nations* are in such close and incessant mutual communion that none can be indifferent to any important change occurring in another. It is saying too little to say that they exist next to each other. If they are to subsist, they must subsist with each other and through each other. Upon this indispensable communion the whole European international law is founded . . .[5]

Metternich served the needs of his state. The multinational Danube monarchy had little to gain by war and would dissolve if militant nationalism triumphed. Is it logical to scorn or minimize his work for peace just because it was to Austria's interest? In the long run, is not peace to every country's interest? In this instance, did not the interests of Austria and of a war-weary Europe usually coincide?

There were certain Austrian chauvinists who did not think the interests always coincided. Even Gentz, an enthusiastic antichauvinist, once lamented the excessive substitution of "Europe" for "Austria" in Metternichian diplomacy. This reproach, which Austria's Foreign Minister refused to appease, was heard more than once from the Imperial entourage. An example is the German nationalist, Archduke John. His intrigues, along with those of Archduchess Sophia, allegedly did more from above to topple Metternich in 1848 than did the open enemies from below.[6] So much the better for the cause of internationalism that Metternich was never a thorough Austrian—though he became a thorough Viennese, something quite different and more cosmopolitan. Decisive is the fact that he grew to manhood as a Rhinelander, steeped in French culture; a Romanized German; a European.

Metternich was not inflexibly the "Don Quixote of legitimacy," as the Viennese poet Grillparzer called him in a witty epitaph.[7] Insofar as legitimacy meant making sacred cows of the reigning family, it was less a principle of Metternich's than a stratagem of Talleyrand's, as agent of the Bourbon restoration, to make France internationally respectable again. Dynastic legitimacy was ignored at Vienna when it came to the German princelings expropriated by Napoleon or the retention of the Swedish throne by the plebeian General Bernadotte. But insofar as the spirit of legitimacy meant the exaltation of law, it was inseparable from Metternich's conservative internationalism. In 1825, he argued that "the moral essence of the Alliance" lay in the duty of the individual states to *"submit to the common law."* This principle "exists everywhere" for states and individuals; without it, he concluded, there can be no peace and no "social body."[8]

G. Ferrero's well known *Reconstruction of Europe* (N.Y., 1941) remains the best defense of legitimism as a concept. The only reason that valuable book has not been drawn upon as a source in the present pages is that the Ferrero book is mainly devoted to Talleyrand's rather than Metternich's use of legitimism. And in view of Talleyrand's very different policies before 1815, his use of the word and concept seems—in contrast with Metternich's—a mere gimmick, to get France out of a tough spot, rather than a rooted, substantial philosophy of conservatism.

For Metternich every force, including the nascent nationalism and the nascent capitalism, must submit to outside laws. This philosophy met its defeat in one that arose in Germany in his own time, one that can best be described as the metaphysics of *Volk,* the religion of nationalism. What do the Germans mean by *Volk?* We can start off by calling it a force. In the French Revolution it awoke, and its name was *la patrie.* In the spiritual revolution of German romanticism, it gained self-consciousness: this self-consciousness was the nation. To the romantics the culture, the symbolic myths, even the folk songs they collected were not produced by individuals but by this impersonal collective force. The *Volk* was a mysteriously indivisible unit, never to be found in the sum of the individuals composing it, just as Rousseau's fantastic "General Will" exceeded his "Will of All."

In a universe governed by Euclid's law that the whole is no greater than the sum of its parts, these doctrines are sheer mysticism, frankly and proudly. The *Volk* does not, can not possibly exist. Yet the fanatic belief in its existence, heralded by Arndt, Jahn, Fichte, and Richard Wagner, is the key factor in all German history after 1848.

A pure force is completely self-determined. Its only righteousness is its self-fulfilment. Its only wrong is its compromise or frustration. It no more obeys the laws of morality than those of Euclid. Under the spell of pride, hate, and demagogy, it sweeps away like burst chains all laws outside itself, all hampering objective principles. But it was the latter Metternich strove to uphold.

No wonder the great Austrian conservative did not inspire the hearts of the German or Italian masses. Yet without some external discipline, like the framework of the Hapsburg state, the new force was doomed to self-destruction. Once each nationalism was no longer limited by an international code or an international dynasty, its own self-preservation meant the destruction of rival nationalisms, the war of all against all.

Metternich saw only stark madness in the concept of the state as an indivisible organic unit, where all individuals and classes and the whole government melted together into a sacred *Volk.* At the same time as he rejected this specious synthesizing of the romantic nationalists, he transcended the mechanistic analysis of the rootless liberals by building on the reality of tradition. Because of this traditionalism he remained, in his phrase, *"tout à terre, tout historique."*

Yet a sense of history was not enough when it came to the politics of the future: mass-politics. This is beyond the power of a diplomat, "who deserved to govern Europe as long as Europe deserved to be governed by diplomacy."[9] What caused his strength in the old Europe, caused his weakness in the new. Grillparzer protested, "How lacking in grandeur his outlook has always been, narrowly fastened upon cabinets and unaware that the time of national mass-politics [*Völkerpolitik*] has arrived."[10]

The time had arrived for the politics of *Volk*. Subjective, recognizing no objective principles outside its own force, mystical and unrealistic to the core, the politics of *Volk* found its natural tool in the self-styled *Realpolitik*. *Realpolitik* is force-politics, the opposite of "Force within Law." It is really nothing positive but a despair of anything better, a lack of faith in any universal code of good and bad. It is most beneath good and evil when it tries hardest to be "beyond good and evil," in the romanticist Faustian hoax of the "daemonic" *(das daemonische)*. Its only pretense of positive justification is an old-fashioned, pseudoscientific pseudo-Darwinism, applying "survival of the fittest" to nations, nations being—here its romanticism comes out—like "organisms." The concept of the organic is basic to every form of German romanticism. Not only *Volk* but the state (in Adam Müller's philosophy), the individual ego, nature, life, and God (as in Schelling's pantheistic *Gott-Natur*) are each in some romantic system considered as a ceaselessly evolving, organic whole. This whole, in all these systems, is a synthesis which cannot be analyzed into parts nor limited by any law outside its organic oneness.

Like the statesmen of nationalist force-politics, if less crudely, Metternich numbered diplomatic deviousness among his social accomplishments. But unlike his successors, his theory and practice did at least follow certain universal grooves, valid for all Europe. Since the triumph of *Realpolitik* in the age of the mass-man, Europe has followed no grooves at all. Or grooves leading to head-on collisions.

It is often forgotten that Metternich did not set foot in Vienna till the age of 22, as a Rhenish refugee from the

French invasion. Only then did he become "central European," linked to the Hapsburg union of east with west. His outlook could not help being international in the mellow 18th-century manner. He belonged to the aristocracy, in itself an international trade union. He felt solidarity with the elements of stability and traditionalism in all countries. His relatives, his friends, and his *petites* friends were as mixed in their national origins as his famous wine cellar. He was at home in all capitals; and perhaps in no suburbs. Italy was his favorite place of relaxation. He was steeped in the philosophy and literature of France, Germany, and England: in the lachrymose fashion of his day, he and Gentz would weep over the poems of Byron and Heine, but the German romantic school he dismissed as "an antiliterature."[11] He spoke several languages and generally wrote in French.

With such a background of easygoing cosmopolitan tolerance on the part of Metternich and his fellow diplomats at the Congress of Vienna, the victors were emotionally capable of international reconciliation, in contrast with the nationalist vengeance of most peace conferences. In a letter to Louis XVIII in 1815, Talleyrand rejoiced—this was before Napoleon's Hundred Days—that the French people were not forced to pay reparations although Napoleon had always forced neighboring countries to pay for his armies. Territorially France was not violated. Even after her embarrassing lapse of the Hundred Days, she was allowed to keep more than her original boundaries of 1789. For several reasons:

Most conservatives wanted to reroot the Bourbons in a country eroded by revolution. To make them sign a tough peace would have made them as unpopular "back home" as later the Weimar Republic. (But one must be on guard lest the valid objection to a tough peace be perverted into an apology or explanation for Nazism, which took the undoubted defects of Versailles as a propaganda-pretext against Weimar but was caused less by Versailles than by the antiwestern and antirational metapolitics of Germany's 19th-century nationalists.) Tsar Alexander was so thoroughly educated in French culture that he knew far more French history than Russian history. Long in touch with the secret anti-Bonaparte underground of Talleyrand, Alexander proclaimed the Allies had been fighting the French dictator, not the French people. Talleyrand further increased the bargaining power of his defeated country through the Allied split in 1814 of Russia and Prussia against Austria and England over the division of Saxony and Poland. Metternich wanted to insure peace by leaning over backwards to avoid inciting French nationalism to a war of *révanche*. England's Castlereagh, whom Metternich called his "alter ego,"[12] also agreed to this: "No arrangement could be wise that carried ruin to one of the countries between which it was concluded."

Castlereagh stressed what America forgot in its one-sided demobilization of 1945: the need to maintain the western half of what he called the "just equilibrium" of peace in order to avoid tempting Russia to further expansion.

France was allowed to keep Alsace-Lorraine by the peace-builders of 1815. She was stripped of Alsace-Lorraine by the nationalist breeders of future war in 1871. They had been anticipated by the German nationalists at the Congress of Vienna, headed by Stein, who demanded that these two provinces be annexed to a powerful, centralized German Confederation. This was also demanded by the influential Francophobe newspaper *Der Rheinische Merkur,* edited by the German nationalist Görres. The *Merkur* was often used to broadcast Stein's policies and to bring popular pressure against the Vienna diplomats.

Metternich's publicist Gentz, countering Stein's publicists, sent the *Merkur* a rebuttal which still remains one of the most persuasive documents of what we today would call the United Nations spirit. He reminded the booty-craving nationalists, as a fellow ally, that the purpose of a peace conference is to restore peace. A lasting peace must reconcile the loser as well as the victor to the new order. As if foreseeing the results of 1871, Gentz argued that the proposed dismemberment of France would produce hate and future wars to the ruin of all parties concerned.

On this issue, Stein lost and Metternich won. Talleyrand's above-mentioned letter to his King concluded that France "was treated with a moderation of which no perusal of history furnishes examples in similar circumstances." At Charlemagne's international capital of Aix-la-Chapelle in 1818, the admission of France on an equal basis converted the Quadruple Alliance against Napoleon and revolution into a Quintuple Alliance for peace and conservatism. By this act, Castlereagh and Metternich together lifted Europe above warring national hatreds. We must "try if we can," Castlereagh had announced earlier at the Congress of Vienna, "to bring back the world to peaceful habits."[13]

Under Bismarck, Germany finally took the Prussian rather than the Austrian path. Until then, the choice remained. The contrast between Stein and Metternich symbolizes that choice. A mutual personal loathing accompanied the contrast in impersonal principles. The earnest and heavy Stein declared, "I have no confidence . . . in the shallow and frivolous Metternich." In turn, the "Adonis of the salons" (to use the ultimate in sarcasm by the pro-Stein historian Treitschke) listed Stein with Chateaubriand and Canning as a "class of people" against whom "my feelings instinctively rebel."

The two men were not dissimilar in origins, being aristocratic Rhinelanders. The contrast appeared when the one gravitated to Berlin, the other to Vienna. The contrast deepened in their attitudes toward the German "War of Liberation" against France. Both played prominent rôles in it, and each considered it the crowning achievement of his own diplomacy. In reality they were fighting two different wars. Metternich's was a war of diplomats: to restore the oneness of Europe and to end revolution. Stein's was a war of peoples: to destroy Napoleon by nationalist revolution and to build a new world of national states. Metternich's was an international civil war; Stein's was a national war between a virtuous Germany and a diabolical France.

As Prussia's modernizer and a sincere liberal reformer, Stein was a great statesman, incomparably greater in this respect than Metternich. Yet Stein's reforms turned out to be but tools to serve Prussian militarism and German nationalism. For Metternich nationalism and Jacobinism were almost identical: twin aspects of the same anticonservative heresy, and equally fatal to the multinational Hapsburg union. Distrusting Stein's direct appeals to the German masses, Metternich claimed that "the revolutionary spirit" hid "under the veil of patriotism." "Hatred of the military despotism of Bonaparte" could so easily pass into hatred of "the legitimate power of their masters."[14]

Metternich feared and fought the hysteria of the middle-class university students, these "national Jacobins" who applauded Stein, Arndt, Görres, Father Jahn, and Field Marshal Blücher and who volunteered for the fanatic war of hate against France preached by these leaders. Hate against France could so easily pass into a revolt against western civilization in general, a repetition of the heathen Saxon revolt against Charlemagne or of the battle of Teutoburg Forest of 9 A.D., in which the Germanic tribes of Hermann defeated the legions of Augustus and prevented Romanization and westernization from crossing the Rhine. The Francophobe playwright Kleist helped to substantiate these fears by his drama *The Battle of Hermann (Die Hermannschlacht)*.

Kleist happens to be Germany's greatest romantic dramatist. His undoubted esthetic genius qualified him for politics about as much as did Richard Wagner's or Ezra Pound's. Written in 1808 and published posthumously in 1826, his *Battle of Hermann* implied that German Kultur must resist France's civilization just as it had once resisted Rome's. This minor work of a major artist sounds as if written by a Nazi in 1939 instead of 1808. Hermann is pictured as a German Führer. His warriors appeal not to Christ but to the nordic Wotan for victory. "Falseness" is defined as the opposite of "blond hair and blue eyes." The play reflects the same new religion of *Volk* that inspired Fichte the very same year in his *Speeches to the German Nation*. Kleist glorifies Hermann for tricking Emperor Augustus (symbolizing French culture and Emperor Napoleon) in a sort of Munich Pact peace and then suddenly massacring the effete overcivilized westerners.

This politically influential drama was, of course, included in a popular Kleist edition under Hitler. The Nazi editor summarizes it as "revenge for suffered wrongs," on an analogy with Hitler's revenge against Versailles: "For this requirement every human restraint and convention must be withdrawn, even the laws of humanity. The poet considers *all means justified* for Hermann, even lies and deception—the offer of an alliance to Augustus—in order to reach the holy goal, the liberation of Germania from the Roman yoke." In further comparison with Hitler, the editor concludes that Germans must regard Hermann as a "noble hero, although to reach his goal he is treacherous and cruel."[15] What links Nazism and Stalinism and forever separates them from western civilization is precisely this antiethics, this justifying of means by end, this flouting of those "general laws" of humanity "to which all alike can look for salvation in adversity" (to cite once more from Thucydides the basic axiom of conservatism).

Like Jahn, the liberal Arndt, the composer Richard Wagner, and so many other anti-Metternich rebels of 1819 or 1848 in Germany, Kleist was also an anti-Semite. Hate of the Jews, as "un-German" and "international," was prophetically frequent among many of the liberals, radicals, and nationalists whom Metternich fought as the "demagogue" movement and whose outlook reached Hitler via Wagner. Despite his anti-conservatism, the rebel poet Heinrich Heine remarked in 1823: "Although I am a Radical in England and a Carbonarist in Italy, I am no Demagogue in Germany for the entirely accidental and trifling reason that, with the triumph of the latter, several thousand Jewish heads, and precisely the best ones, would fall."[16] In contrast with his opinion of these German anti-Metternichians, Heine had some relatively good words for his political enemy Metternich, an internationalist to whom racial prejudice was nonsense. "I have a certain feeling of tenderness," wrote Heine, "for Metternich" who "can never in his heart love servility and obscurantism."[17] He was at least "an open, honest enemy" of liberalism (added Heine later) who never "made us indignant through private malice" but acted "not out of petty hate but loftily in the spirit of a system to which Austria has remained faithful for 300 years."[18]

Is it being unhistorical to judge the anti-Metternichian nationalism and racism of 19th-century Germany by its Nazi consequences? Were these consequences the logical outcome or a modern accident for which nationalism should not be blamed? Is it a case of the wise-after-the-event fallacy to read so much into these early rebels of 1806-1848, whom many historians still consider great liberals? The answer is that certain disregarded contemporaries of this liberal nationalism were wise long before the event, and them nobody can accuse of reading a later Nazism into an earlier nationalism, for they lived a century before Hitler.

As if foreseeing the influence of Wagner's unborn Nibelungen operas on an unborn Führer, Goethe feared that the romantic revival of Siegfried legends might lead to an anticivilized glorification of that early warlike Teutonic barbarism. The liberal Heine, an opponent of the Metternich system, feared infinitely more the new anti-Metternichian ideology of a mystical German nationalism. He can hardly be accused of writing after 1933. Yet he demonstrated logically, in his extraordinary essay on German philosophy, that a world-menacing anti-Christian religion was arising from the romantics, by which he meant the egoistical subjective idealism, nationalism, and "fanaticism of the Will" of the Fichte school and what he called "the Nature philosophers." "These doctrines," wrote Heine in 1834, "have developed revolutionary forces which only await the day to break forth and fill the world with terror and astonishment."[19]

At the time, Metternich had successfully repelled some new outbreaks by the various brands of German nationalist and antimonarchist rebels, all still lumped together as "the liberals" in most histories. In his essay, Heine consoled the revolutionists with bitter irony by proving that the thwarted German revolution was bound to triumph at some future date and that its violence and nihilism would make other western revolutions, such as that of 1789, mere milk-and-water affairs in comparison. The German "Nature" cult would have "terrible" results because its atavistic return to the "primitive powers of Nature" would "evoke the demoniac energies of old German pantheism." This anticipates the quotation from Albert Guérard: "The romantic rebellion against discipline . . . the disastrous surge of the elemental . . . the apologists of dynamic chaos . . . have pushed the world back into chaos."

What would this political sublimation of the romantic school, seemingly so harmless in its fogs of "deep" philosophy, finally bequeath to the world? Heine's answer was: "that brutal German joy in battle . . . that battle-madness which we find among the ancient Teutonic races, who fought for the very love of fighting." Watching Jahn's crusaders march by like Storm Troopers, the author Heinrich Steffens feared that "this vague German patriotism was taking on a *religious* character and becoming ever more threatening."[20] And in 1834 it is precisely this new non-Christian religiosity that Heine detected in the nationalism most German liberals espoused. One hundred years before Hitler, Heine took a look at Hitler's 19th-century antecedents and predicted the outcome:

> Should the subduing talisman, the Cross, break, then will come roaring forth the wild madness of the old champions, the insane Berserker rage, of which the northern poets sing. That talisman is brittle, and the day will come when it will pitifully break. The old stone gods will rise from the long-forgotten ruin and rub the dust of a thousand years from their eyes; and Thor, leaping to life with his giant hammer, will crush the Gothic cathedrals!

If this is what such intelligent Germans as Goethe and Heine were thinking, then Metternich's fears of German nationalism were not so groundless and bigoted as is still commonly believed. He blamed the Wartburg riots of 1817 (public book-burnings, then guided from afar by Jahn and later praised and imitated by Goebbels) and the Kotzebue assassination of 1819 (by the nationalist Karl Sand, a frenzied student-acquaintance of Jahn's) upon the hysteria aroused by Stein, Fichte, Arndt, Jahn, and the nationalistic universities. His Carlsbad Decrees struck back: certainly no executions, but a harmful censorship, snooping, and prying, such as also disgraced our own free society in the Red Scare of the 1920's.

Stein himself, as the most popular hero of both the nationalist and the liberal bourgeoisie, had to be treated with kid gloves, though even he was apparently subjected to a certain amount of surveillance. The hardest blows fell on the proto-Nazi Jahn (jailed for several years, only to return triumphantly in the Revolution of '48), on Arndt (who, though remaining free, lost his job), on the secret nationalist student societies (dissolved, with the universities subject to the tribunal at Mainz), and on such books as Fichte's chauvinistic *Speeches to the German Nation* (new editions discouraged). Milksop measures by totalitarian standards. But rigorous for a Metternich. And disgraceful according to our western standards, whether liberal or conservative.

The more rigorous actions were usually carried out by others, by the German Diet, or by King Frederick William III of Prussia. It was not Metternich nor Austria but Prussia who put Jahn in jail. Yet the heavier responsibility is Metternich's, for the Diet and King Frederick William were following his promptings.

This responsibility, for better or worse, he freely accepted. Foreseeing the threat to a just society of Jahn's secret network of student nationalists, the internationalist Metternich swore to free Germany from what he called *"the dictatorship of such men as Jahn and Arndt."*[21] Earlier, the contrast Metternich-Stein had symbolized the choice between internationalism and nationalism in the Alsace-Lorraine crisis. Half a decade later, the contrast Metternich-Jahn symbolized certain similar aspects of the German crisis. Though ignored in America and England, where his biographies have not even been translated, Jahn is of extraordinary importance as the new type of anti-Metternichian German, that transitional type in whom nationalism for the first time becomes "Nazism." Here the word "Nazism" is not being used loosely nor with retroactive distortion but in the strictest and most accurate sense.[22]

Arndt was no ruffian demagogue like Jahn but a political philosopher who tried to combine a timid liberalism with an aggressive nationalism. The students adored Arndt's well-written hymns of hate against France and his eloquence about a future Germany with more territorial annexations and more unity and more soldiers—but also more liberal and enlightened institutions. This is familiar enough, still in the gentlemanly tradition of Stein. Being still mixed up with liberalism, such nationalism, though far more studied in the English-speaking world, has less significance for what happened in 1933 than Jahn's totalitarianism. The innovator was Father Jahn.

Jahn's organized gangs, praised by a contemporary nationalist as "the Storm Troopers" of a future nationalist seizure of power,[23] roamed the streets molesting citizens who looked "un-German."[24] It is Jahn who coined Hitler's favorite word, *Volkstum* (folkdom), in a book using that title. It means the *Volk* way of life, organically integrated within one's own nationality and race, the sharpest contrast to Metternich's internationalism. A parliamentary committee of Metternich's German Diet classified Jahn's book *German Folkdom* of 1810 with Fichte's *Speeches* of 1808 as "the spiritual godfathers of the newer Germany."[25] A more recent German authority calls Jahn and Arndt "the popularizers of the *Volk*-soul."[26]

Most American and English studies, being based on the rosy assumption that German liberals stood for the same as western liberals, have created a false impression by treating all anti-Metternichians indiscriminately as "persecuted liberals." The word "liberal" is commonly used for Jahn, too. Yet Jahn—and later, Richard Wagner[27]—are the two 19th-century Germans in whose writings the entire Nazi ideology appears point by point, long before any Treaty of Versailles. There is a reason why western historians, with a liberal 19th-century outlook, have so long overlooked this. Their outlook did not prepare them to recognize the seeds of something so different, so sweepingly antiwestern and un-19th century. As Alfred Bäumler, a Nazi author, recognized, "Only the overthrow of the 19th century by National Socialism has enabled us to see freely and purely the figure of Jahn." Or as the Nazi historian Bungardt wrote in 1938, "In Jahn arose another world, a new human type."[28]

Metternich wanted peace and a world-state. In the Concert of Europe he made his ideal work. Jahn, a militarist drill-sergeant, wanted unlimited national sovereignty, unmixed national culture, and unmixed blood. He even suggested setting up a wild no man's land between Germany and France for this purpose. And he protested that the Metternichian concept of a world-state would bring about "the last day of humanity,"²⁹ anticipating a curiously similar passage in *Mein Kampf*. In 1814 he called for a "unity-creator," an unparliamentary dictator, as Führer ("the *Volk* will honor him as savior and forgive him all his sins"). Less squeamish about bloody means than any Metternich, Jahn wanted this future Führer to burn out antinational provincialism in Germany by Hippocrates' cure for cancer: "What medicine does not heal is healed by iron; what iron does not heal is healed by fire."³⁰ Here the triumph of "blood and iron" is anticipated by half a century.

By 1815 Jahn was permanently wearing the "true German costume" of his own invention. He wanted all Germans to wear this national uniform,³¹ a homespun anticipation of Germany's recent Brownshirt costume. Thus clad, Jahn had only recently been swaggering through the streets of conquered Paris. After Bonaparte's fall, Jahn had entered the French capital in the entourage of Prussian officials. They encouraged him, though only temporarily, because he was a sturdy annexationist propagandist in the dispute between Stein and Metternich about France. With his long beard flowing in the wind (he claimed it had turned gray from horror when France won the battle of Jena),³² Father Jahn harangued crowds on the need for things natural, primitive, and Teuton. Typical of the glorification of lawlessness and violence in this whole movement is his pride in vandalism: he clambered up the Arc de Triomphe to knock the tuba from the mouth of the goddess of victory.

Gleefully he quoted French journals which dubbed him "Chief of the Corps of Vengeance." What a contrast this grotesque figure made at the Congress of Vienna with the suave diplomats of conservatism like Castlereagh and Metternich.³³ Though they considered Jahn an uproarious joke at the time, he was no longer a joke for Metternich only four years later at Carlsbad. Unhappily for Europe, the future was to belong to Jahn and not to the conservatives.

While most of Europe after 1815 shared Metternich's desire for peace, Jahn was thundering, "Germany needs a war of her own in order to feel her power; she needs a feud with Frenchdom to develop her national way of life in all its fullness. This occasion will not fail to come . . ."[34] It came in 1870, in 1914, and in 1940, ever since Bismarck discovered that an anti-French crusade was the best way to unify and militarize Germany. The second best way was by turning German education into a system of propaganda and indoctrination of youth. This totalitarian method of education was advocated by Jahn with real psychological insight and is partly his invention. Hitler's educational system was "in part the legacy of Jahn. . . . When Hitler speaks of . . . history as the science which demonstrates that one's own people is always right, he is echoing Jahn."[35]

The Nazi purge of foreign words was also borrowed from Jahn's program. He helped found Germany's first "Language Purification Society." Because "university," for example, is a word of un-Nordic Latin origin, one of Jahn's disciples replaced it with the expression "Institute of Mental Gymnastics."[36] Incensed that un-Nordic French was the normal language of Metternichian international aristocracy, Jahn shouted in a lecture-hall of 1817, "The father who lets his daughter learn French is just as good as the man who apprentices his daughter to whoredom."[37] Elsewhere he wailed, "Unhappy Germany, neglect of your mother tongue has been fearfully avenged upon you. . . . This language [French] has rendered impotent your men, led your children astray, and dishonored your wives."[38]

Those who think the Aryan cult began with Gobineau, may be surprised by Jahn's anti-Semitic diatribes or by his appeals for biological *Volk* purity. His book *Folkdom* made such a battle cry of German purity and superiority that Field Marshal Blücher, the Francophobe co-conqueror of Napoleon at Waterloo, praised it as the verbal equivalent of a gun.[39] Sample quotations: "Animal hybrids have no genuine power of propagation, and hybrid peoples have just as little posterity." "The purer a people, the better; the more mixed, the worse." "A state without a *Volk* is nothing, a soulless artifice. A *Volk* without a state is nothing, a lifeless frivolous phantom like the vagabond gypsies and Jews."[40] Like so many of Metternich's war-loving foes, Jahn urged Germany to annex the Danes, Dutch, and Swiss as blood-brothers.[41] This combination of racism and *Lebensraum* was not to be fulfilled till Hitler's temporary conquest of Denmark and Holland and his gas chambers for Jahn's "vagabond gypsies and Jews."

To conceal his proto-Nazi political radicalism, Jahn disguised his youth movement as an innocent society for gymnastic exercises. Spreading rapidly, the gymnast craze reached its peak in 1817, the year of the Wartburg disorders, with 1,074 paticipants in Berlin itself. Important is the fact that many of these young gymnasts had fought as volunteers against France in the famous Free Corps of 1813, which Jahn had done so much to organize. He had enlisted, equipped, and helped train enough men for a full battalion—one-third of the entire Free Corps![42] When these middle-class youths returned to their interrupted studies, Jahn's hold on German universities tightened, as shown by the fact that in 1817 two important universities gave him an honorary degree.[43] Influenced by Stein, Fichte, Arndt, Jahn, and the *Burschenschaften,* the German university was by the time of Carlsbad the stronghold of nationalist opposition to Metternich and to the boundaries of 1815.

The gymnast camouflage did not deceive the Austrian Foreign Minister. In 1818 Metternich warned Prussia: "The gymnastic institution is the real training ground for the university mischief. . . . The inventor [Jahn], the invention, and the execution come from Prussia. . . . The lower institutions are like the branch lodges of a mother lodge. One has to grasp the evil by the roots."[44] In the battle between Metternich and the Jahn movement, the Carlsbad Decrees were such a grasp at evil's "roots." But they also struck at much that was wholesome and truly liberal in the western sense. An attempt to suppress ideas, even evil ideas, is in any case a morally dubious solution.

Persuaded by Metternich's warnings about the Jahn movement, the King of Prussia finally closed down the gymnastic fields.[45] Not until after Jahn's imprisonment were they reopened again. The Prussian courts jailed him on charges of revolutionary conspiracy.[46] Thus ended the Jahn-Metternich duel: first chapter in the fascist-nationalist revolution against both conservative internationalism and liberal nationalism. It is perhaps too much to hope that the last chapter ended when Alfred Rosenberg, Hitler's Director of Weltanschauung, was hanged at Nuremberg in 1945. Loathing Metternichian internationalism for postponing Germany's Nazi destiny, Rosenberg cited as leitmotif for his book on "The Coming Reich" the words on *Volk* of Father Jahn.[47]

To Metternich the hotheads around Stein, Arndt, and Jahn were not his allies against French Jacobins so much as they were themselves a kind of unintentional Jacobin: "national Jacobins" or "German Jacobins" was what Metternich and other conservatives called them.[48] Useful in winning the war against Metternich's enemy, Napoleon, were the three related emotions of hate, war fervor, and nationalism. Therefore, Metternich was expected to be grateful for the aid rendered by such "psychological warfare," as many Prussian officials were. But for him the end did not justify such means. Here is his final verdict on the War of Liberation: "Prussia committed a grave fault in calling to her aid such dangerous weapons."[49] His use of the word "dangerous" in this passage was considered by critics the wild overstatement of a reactionary slandering progress. "Dangerous" is a mild understatement compared to Heine's prophecy ("insane Berserker rage") and Hitler's fulfilment.

During Metternich's hegemony, Europe was spared Thor's "giant hammer." The German Confederation, founded and guided by Metternich, gave Germany unity but a loose unity. This sufficed for peace. It sufficed for defense against France. Being decentralized and unmilitarized, it did not suffice for those who wanted aggressive wars to annex blood-brothers and enslave Slavs. The one thing on which the wrangling liberals of 1848 agreed was military coercion of non-Germans in the mixed border-areas. In June, 1848 the liberal assembly at Frankfort am Main, elected by universal suffrage during the revolution, backed the Austrian military suppression of Czech liberals. On July 27, 1848 Frankfort similarly voted to back the Prussian army's suppression of the government set up by Polish liberals in Posen. Building the first national navy in

Germany's history, the assembly also began an abortive war with Denmark over Schleswig-Holstein.

The hour had come when these liberal nationalists had to stop straddling: they must choose between nationalism first or liberalism first. There ensued no long Hamlet-like hesitation.

The racially tolerant Metternich had not persecuted non-Germans for their different culture or language. In 1848, the Frankfort coercion of Slavs paralleled that of the Budapest revolution in the same year. The intolerant liberals and leftists of Kossuth tried to Magyarize the hapless Slavs of Croatia and to force them to speak only Hungarian in the new "democratic" parliament. Not surprisingly, the Croats fought for their Hapsburg emperor against these liberals in the civil war that followed. From Budapest and Frankfort, Croats and Czechs learned the same lesson the hard way: the need to halt national aggressiveness by means of an international union of the Hapsburgs. This union Metternich had maintained. The post-Metternich ministries of Austria upset the balance too far against Zagreb and Prague in favor of Budapest. The price was 1918. So died Danubia.

The liberal university professors, Metternich's fiercest foes and now so prominent in 1848, were often far from the cloudy idealists pictured in our textbooks. From his own viewpoint, Bismarck erred in mocking their lack of *Realpolitik*. The majority that voted for the Prussian army on July 27 was more Bismarckian than Bismarck ever realized. Many liberals, for example Treitschke, later became leading propagandists for Bismarck, along with the new National Liberal Party. Only an honorable few continued to oppose him and the militarist success-worship that followed his victorious wars. In fairness to western liberals, it may be noted that a truly great liberal like Mill repudiated the persecuting nationalism of eastern liberals,[50] just as most western conservatives repudiated the intolerant tsarist conservatives.

How did the German liberals reconcile with democratic principles the fact of the Czech majority in Bohemia and the Polish majority in Posen if these two provinces were to be reconquered and Germanized? The answer was alluringly simple: might makes right, and democracy is best served when superior Germans teach inferior aliens their place. This solution was freely voted by a large majority of these liberals and anti-Metternich revolutionists after the all-important Polish debate of July, 1848. In March, the Frankfort assembly still expressed international liberal sympathies for all races, specifically including the Poles. The Polish debate of July 24-27 was the turning-point for German liberalism and for the post-Metternich history of central Europe. After this debate—the quotations that follow may be found in its stenographic records—the assembly supported the Prussian army against the Polish provinces needed for *Lebensraum*.

In this decision the assembly followed the influential liberal leader from East Prussia, 29-year-old William Jordan, overwhelming the more tolerant minority led by Robert Blum of Saxony. The learned young Jordan (1819-1904) was a man of contradictions; a sincere constitutional liberal, at the same time a Hegelian philosopher of Prussianism; also a poet, whose later epic *Die Nibelungen* has been overshadowed by Wagner's opera on that most Germanic of subjects.

In May, 1848 Jordan became Secretary of the Naval Affairs Committee of the young revolution. In the July debate, in a popular speech that at once became famous, he attacked as treason to the fatherland any cosmopolitan regard for the rights of the Polish majority in Posen. Urging the right of the German minority as the right of the stronger, he praised Prussia's mission of conquering a backward east with Teuton sword and plough. To his applauding hearers, his eloquence conveyed the ecstasy of German power and the glory of brutal ruthlessness when needed as means to this end.[51]

His orations[52] include the following premises, prophetic of Hitler. The superior power of Germanic stock over Slavic stock is a phenomenon of natural history which cannot be altered by the decrees of abstract cosmopolitan ideas of justice.[53] Posen is less a question of oppressed nationalities than of German national security; the solution is a "healthy national egoism."[54] "Freedom for all; but the power and welfare of the fatherland above all"[55]—with this interesting sentence, he evidently tried to find the formula reconciling the contradiction between international liberalism and liberal nationalism.

Like Arndt and Jahn, now hailed at Frankfort as aging

eagles, young Jordan was one of the first articulate Pan-Germans. He was one of the first prophets of *Realpolitik* as the means to the Pan-German goal. This broke not only with Metternich's internationalism. It broke with the tolerant peaceful nationalism of Herder and Mazzini, to whom all nationalities were equal in rights. Jordan, in contrast, insisted on inequality. Like Fichte he insisted that the pure German *Volk* had a special world mission.

On January 11, 1849, in another important speech to the assembly, he argued that this mission was to Germanize other races. He had the Slavic east especially in mind. But Pan-Germanism also faces west. The same speech denounced the loss of Alsace to France as shameful.[56] This echoed the Stein-Metternich debate of 1815 and anticipated Bismarck's annexation of Alsace in 1871 and Hitler's in 1940. Already in 1848 Jordan foresaw the Bismarck solution to German unity. Prussia's mission, proclaimed Jordan, was to unify Germany by war if necessary, even against Austria and even though this might mean "a deluge of blood."[57]

Healthy national egoism, right of the stronger, and deluge of blood: "In these phrases, welcomed by the liberal majority, the Frankfort liberals delivered themselves to the Prussian Army and, by an inevitable logic, delivered German liberalism first to Bismarck and later to Hitler."[58]

Such were the Good Democrats who liberated Europe from Metternich. But the "healthy" nationalism of these patriotic liberals was to be their own death warrant when the liberal Weimar Republic failed to defend itself against Hitler with adequate vigor.

After the alarums of 1819, the King of Prussia usually listened more to Metternich than to the German nationalists. Until the Bismarckian "transvaluation of all values," Austria and not Prussia set the pace in Germany. Metternich's restraint of Prussia, in effect till 1848, was not through official coercion but through his unofficial personal tact and prestige. He exerted his influence through coöperation and through prior discussion of any contemplated action, rather than iron fist or *fait accompli*. This policy was the only way to manage the proud heirs of Frederick the Great.

Schwarzenberg, Metternich's successor after the Revolution,

reversed this policy. The reversal epitomized the contrast between "green tables" and "vive la force!" The first law of Metternichian diplomacy was never to win an obvious diplomatic triumph, always to save the opponent's face, never to push it publicly into the dust. A rough and ruthless soldier, who had only recently suppressed Austria's parliament and Hungary's constitution, Schwarzenberg gloated over such triumphs of brute force as Austria's public humiliation of Prussia at Olmütz in 1850.

Bismarck had originally been pro-Austrian. He had even defended the Olmütz abasement because he had opposed German unity ("Prussians we are, and Prussians we shall remain"). At the German Diet after 1851, this tough new Austrian *Realpolitik* towards Prussia continued despite Schwarzenberg's death. It ended Bismarck's faith in Austrian leadership. It convinced him of the need for war and for uniting Germany under Prussia.

His decision is one of the most important in history. It has directly affected America, who suffered in two World Wars from the Prussian solution of the German problem. This solution meant not only the forcible expulsion of Austria in 1866 but an aggressive, Potsdamized, militarized Germany. Was this, as the Treitschke school of Prussian propagandists trumpeted, the inevitable solution for Germany? Or might all this have been prevented if Austria had kept up Metternich's tradition of a more farsighted coöperative diplomacy? *Realpolitik*, being a bomb with a chain reaction, destroys all sides concerned because it provokes its own counteropposition. Schwarzenberg's *Realpolitik* is the now-forgotten parent of Bismarck's. In turn, Bismarck's blood and iron reached its unBismarckian extreme in modern fascist and Stalinist militarism.

From the viewpoint of current national hates, nothing seems less realistic than the Christian world brotherhood proclaimed by the monarchs who signed the Holy Alliance in 1815. Secretly among conservatives and publicly among liberals, the document became a standard joke. This was due to the highfalutin messianic phrasing given it by Tsar Alexander, then studying the supernatural with such charlatan mystics as

Madame Krüdener. Were she living today, she would have made a fortune in southern California and might have received her Guru letters from presidential candidates instead of from tsars.

Castlereagh called the Holy Alliance document "a piece of sublime mysticism and nonsense." Metternich called it a "sonorous nothing," an "overflow of the pietistic feelings of Emperor Alexander." Gentz called it "stage decoration." Clearly it can hardly be taken at face value.[59] But this chorus of irony in high conservative places does not entitle the modern conservative to laugh it off with easy cynicism. Stripped of its old-fashioned monarchic paternalism, the much-mocked document is a sincere appeal for a peaceful brotherhood between all classes and all nations. This makes better sense and better morals than today's less naive and less laughable Unholy Alliance of class war and national war.

Another favorite butt of labored sarcasm is Metternich's reference to Italy as a "geographical expression."[60] This semantically excellent phrase is supposed to unmask his hopeless unprogressiveness at one swoop. Foreseeing the results of exclusively national loyalties, Metternich the educator was building up a Europe where local nations would be mere geographical expressions and where loyalties would be to Europe as a whole. Those most incensed by his epigram about Italy were those who, in turn, dismissed as a geographical expression his Pan-European league. His struggle against their "atavistic attacks of soil attachment" was not only negative and repressive but positive and creative, based on his credo that "Europe has come to be my native country."[61]

In the light of two World Wars of nationalism, we must choose at last: is western man's "native country" to be an ever broadening community of humanity—as Metternich's was "Europe"—or is it to be some narrowly and meanly provincial "nation"? On this choice the great builders of western culture, whether an Alexander the Great or an Erasmus or St. Paul, long ago took their stand. And on this they stand closer to Professor Metternich than to all the Carbonari of Naples or to any Baron vom und zum Stein.

Metternich was a diplomat, not a demagogue. Monarchs, but

not the masses, were his pupils.[62] The Metternich system and the force of *Volk* collided. Because the resulting explosion changed the whole map of Europe, we can understand our own time better by returning to this point of origin. *"Kraft im Recht"*: the Metternichian demand for a universal law above private force is the last best hope not only of internationalism, not only of peace, but perhaps—since Hiroshima—of the survival of man.

Chapter 3

THE CONSERVATIVE
WAY
TO FREEDOM

THE FLAME OF CHRISTIAN ETHICS IS STILL OUR HIGHEST
GUIDE.
—CHURCHILL'S SPEECH OF MARCH 31, 1949

AND ONLY LAW CAN GIVE US FREEDOM.
—FROM GOETHE'S SONNET *Natur und Kunst*

3

Past interpretations usually stress the contrast between the English system and the Metternich system. This contrast does deserve some of its emphasis. On the other hand, there is a basic link between the ideals of Metternich and of English parliamentary government. This is their common evolution from Edmund Burke. Burke was one of those "great oaks," the 18th-century Whigs. Their genius for moral leadership, and for the highest intellectual level of parliamentary debate, deserves to be the model for modern conservative leadership, along with the genius of the 19th-century Tories for blending humane reform with historic continuity.

Today any number of so-called political commentators claim to interpret the news. Americans will find none timelier than Burke though his *Reflections on the Revolution in France* are dated 1790. He teaches us to answer world revolution not by outbidding it with a leftism of our own nor by reactionary rightist tyranny but by conserving the free institutions of the west. We could do worse than model our foreign policy on this earlier victim of the "war monger" label, who believed in international unity against the aggressor and who bluntly told the isolationists of his day what would happen to their own house if they ignored the fire in their neighbor's. To witnesses of the Hitler and Stalin terror, Burke's superlatives against the more amateurish Jacobin terror sound overstated for his own day, as do Metternich's. Instead, the warnings of the Austrian and the Englishman sound as if directed to us today. Burke, as Crane Brinton reminds us,

> confronted in the French Revolution the kind of challenge we have confronted and still confront in the totalitarian revolutions of our day. He met that challenge by an appeal to the fundamental standards of our western civili-

zation, an appeal which has itself helped clarify and formulate those standards. The debate between Burke and Paine, whose famous "Rights of Man" was a pamphlet in reply to Burke's "Reflections on the French Revolution," has been decided in favor of Burke as clearly as the debate over the relation between the motions of sun and earth has been decided in favor of Copernicus. . . . Anyone brought up in the Christian tradition should from the start be proof against the great error Burke spent his life combating, namely that human beings are born naturally good and naturally reasonable.[1]

Burke's writings were introduced to central Europe by Metternich's friend and chief assistant, Friedrich Gentz. In his youth a radical pro-Jacobin journalist, Gentz went through the usual disillusionment, influenced by his own experiences as well as by Burke, whom he translated into German. Gentz became the Hapsburg empire's spokesman for discipline and common sense—and an undisciplined prey to his passion for bonbons, actresses, and the lyrics of the unconservative Heine. Metternich probably owes many of his Burkean political insights to Gentz, who as secretary of the Congress of Vienna became "Secretary of Europe."[2]

In 1848, like the French Premier Guizot and like Prussia's future William I, it was to England that Metternich fled—as a matter of course. His detractors gloated over the supposed irony of this.[3] The irony was shallow: Austria's champion of peace and order was finding refuge in what, despite Palmerston, remained the world's most peaceful and orderly nation. England's success was a justification, not a disproof, of Metternich's ideas. "The freest land on earth because the best disciplined," he called it.[4] "The English aristocracy is not the noblesse. It consists of the *conservative principles* and of the spirit which answers to them, a spirit animating *all* classes."[5] Without honor in his own country, Metternich wrote from his English exile, "I find myself here in the element in which alone I breathe freely, in an atmosphere where good sense predominates."[6]

His unfinished "Political Testament" reasons, as might be

expected, that liberty rests on order. "Without the base of order," liberty is only a disguise for the ambitions of some selfish group. "Viewed as 'constitution,' the best order for a state will be what responds to the material and moral conditions determining the national character. There is no universal recipe for constitutions."[7] Central Europe was not yet ripe for a great deal more freedom, whether governed by republican liberals or by kings, because it lacked the traditions of voluntary order. The new constitutions advocated by the liberals could only cause anarchy because they were no more than words and good intentions. In politics as in literature and psychology, Metternich would have agreed with Goethe's epigram about classical restraint vs. romantic impulse:

"Everything that liberates the spirit without a corresponding growth in self-mastery is pernicious."

Significantly, Goethe responded to Metternich's conservative ideals instead of joining either the liberals or the nationalists in denouncing him. The "good European" of Weimar wrote down his personal impressions of the "good European" of Vienna:

It is encouraging and inspiring to participate in and to be permitted to share the views of such a man who is directing the entire enormous complexity of questions, of which even a fragment would crush us others by its weight. Metternich is one of those who, from the most elevated position of human existence, equipped with the highest possible education, inspires with the assurance that reason, reconciliation, and human understanding will lead us out of present chaos. . . . It is mastered by such able hands![8]

But young liberals were impatient with Goethe as well as with Metternich. They saw only blind despotism when the "Era of Congresses" (1818-22) pulled down the curtain on the comic-opera revolts of tiny minorities in Italy and Spain. So unrepresentative were these overpublicized putsches that the Spanish people, who had fought to the death against the Jacobin French invaders, scarcely resisted and usually welcomed the Bourbon French invaders of 1823. In the abstract and out of context, it is the Italian and Spanish rebels who were in the right, for their goal was democracy and universal bliss. They were not so much "wrong" as irresponsibly unhistorical in trying overnight to force modern middle-class "French ideas" on a semimedieval agricultural community.

Had these liberal doctrinaires of Naples and Cadiz understood Metternich's philosophy of evolutionary growth, they might have rebelled less hastily and slandered his motives less. During these disturbances, he admitted in a letter of 1820 that "moderns" must "go through their young time of lawlessness" but stressed that "man cannot make a constitution, properly speaking," only "time." A merely written constitution is "but a sheet of paper" if not also lived in and grown into. "Just as little is a Charta a constitution as the marriage contract is the marriage;" both must be consummated. He adds that "the Magna Charta is but a subordinate element" of the English constitution. "The English constitution is the work of centuries" rather than the work of a single revolution or a single document or decree. This is why the liberal revolts and liberal decrees failed to strike root in Italy and Spain and were not true to the spirit of the free English institutions that they professed to admire. "What is called a constitution today is nothing but 'get out so that I can get in.' "[9]

While respecting the English constitution as historically adapted to its possessor, Metternich fought the attempts to thrust it by revolution upon the rest of Europe as an artificial cure-all: "Madame de Staël would not find it difficult to show that the weather is bad because the English constitution is not introduced everywhere."[10] To the anarchy caused by such would-be liberators, discipline enforced from above seemed preferable to Metternich. Self-imposed order is best, as England proved. Order imposed from above is only second best. But the difference between a statesman and a fanatic ideologue is that the former knows the humble wisdom of the second best when the best is historically impossible.

At the same time, a great statesman prepares for the best, now impossible but possible in the future. He drew up plans for a parliament and a reformed constitution. In 1832 the Emperor Francis, true to his observation that "the whole world is mad and wants new constitutions," vetoed Metternich's project. The year was a turning-point in world history: the King of England, though not much more liberal than Francis, was meanwhile accepting the Reform Bill of 1832, forestalling for England the fate of the continental monarchies in 1848 and 1918. Lord Grey succeeded where Prince Metternich failed; and where Baron Turgot, whose reforms would have conserved the Bourbon monarchy, had failed before the French Revolution. Though supreme in foreign policy from 1809 to 1848 and though at times dominating all Europe as President of the Congress of Vienna in 1815, Metternich was never supreme in home affairs.

Grey overrode his ruler's objections to the Reform Bill. It is easy for us to condemn Metternich for not having done likewise. But he could not possibly have done so, for Austria was not England; there was no parliament, public opinion, and opposition party to back a dissident minister and curb his king. 1832 is dramatic evidence for our distinction between western and eastern conservatism.

The Paris revolt of 1830 threatened to renew all over Europe the post-1789 duel—mutually destructive—between liberalism and traditional authority. Neither reactionary repression nor radical revolution can end the duel. The solution, as England proved time and again, lies in a patient conservative spirit of mediation between the enlightened but impatient liberals and their legitimate but all too static rulers. Therefore, Metternich, trying hopelessly to persuade his emperor, defended his new constitution of 1832 as *reconciling* "the opposition between the monarchist principles and the democratic."[11] This is the western spirit; this is conservatism at its best, the evolutionary middle way between despots like Francis and the 1848 liberals.

In 1835 the sane and reactionary Francis I was replaced by his son, the feeble-minded and reactionary Ferdinand I. The latter—and archdukes around him—were not too feeble-minded to be able to read and obey; and they read his father's last will and testament, which warned his successor to "displace none of the foundations of the edifice of state. Rule, and change nothing." Even from the grave, Francis foiled Metternich's revolution-preventing compromise and left him as the scapegoat of the revolution.

Metternich was once more at his best when he argued for a parliament by pointing out that the police-state of Francis drove many noble minds into an opposition which, lacking legal means of expression in an unparliamentary absolutism, became revolutionary in appearance. Concluding with a prophecy about what his resignation would bring, Metternich's following statement was not merely wise-after-the-event but was made shortly prior to the Vienna revolution that overthrew him:

> [Emperor Francis] followed my advice in everything on foreign policy. He did not do so in internal affairs. . . . Attributing a perhaps exaggerated importance to the secret societies . . . he thought he found the remedy against the evil in a minute surveillance of the would-be intellectual classes exercised by the police, who thereby became one of the chief instruments of his government; . . . in short, in a moral closing of the frontiers. . . . But it is useless to close the gates against ideas; they overleap them. . . . The result was a dull irritation against the government among the educated classes. I told that to the emperor, but on that point he was unshakeable. All I could do to lessen the grievous results, I did. . . . If in 1817, even as late as 1826, the emperor had adopted my ideas on the reorganization of the diets, we would be perhaps in a position to face the tempest. Today it is too late. . . . My resignation will be the revolution.[12]

Can any liberal disagree with this objective diagnosis of how reaction causes revolution? But can we abstain, no matter how sympathetic to Metternich, from asking ironically: why was there not more energetic action to practice this preaching?

The '48 uprisings were finally put down by the most ruthless dictatorship Austria had ever seen. In contrast, Metternich and even the Francis system now "appeared in a milder light," to quote a significant admission by that Metternich-loathing historian, Bibl.[13] In 1851, Metternich was successfully negotiating his return from exile to Vienna as a private citizen. Though never again to be Minister, he did not abstain from caustic political comment. He warned that the recent policies of Schwarzenberg, whom he called the "unethical diplomat," might lead to a disastrous crisis with "the not yet saturated Prussian state." The observation was acute at a time when Austria was still celebrating her hollow Olmütz triumph over the humiliated Prussians. The concept of saturated and unsaturated nations, adopted by Bismarck after 1871, is commonly considered Bismarck's invention. It was originated by the 79-year-old Metternich when the young Prussian came to chat with him—the future visiting the past—in August, 1851.[14]

If only they had known, liberals would have noted with ironic glee that their enemy was in the 1850's the victim of the same police censorship which had plagued them. The history of this incident, then a secret, is as follows: From time immemorial the Hungarians had claimed the right to a constitution of their own. This right Metternich had helped them to regain during his term of office. After 1848 the Hungarian constitution was again illegally suppressed from Vienna. Back from exile, Metternich issued in printed form his "Aphoristic Remarks" of 1844 about reforming the Hungarian constitution. By such a publication he hoped to influence public opinion. But the Minister of Police intervened to stop this, denouncing the publication as "inopportune" to the new monarch, who joined in condemning it as inflammatory.[15]

Such developments are no surprise if we recall that the Rhinelander Metternich had come as an outsider to Austria. He had always to work within the limits of what he found there, limits he was unable to alter. What he found—the Austria of Francis I—is revealed by a speech the monarch made to a group of professors in 1821:

> Keep yourselves to what is old, for that is good; if our ancestors have proved it to be good, why should not we do as they did? New ideas are now coming forward of which I do not nor ever shall approve. Mistrust these ideas and keep to the positive. I have no need of learned men. I want

faithful subjects. Be such: that is your duty. He who would serve me, must do what I command. He who cannot do this, or who comes full of new ideas, may go his way. If he does not, I shall send him.

Joseph II had predicted of his nephew Francis, "That is a good-for-nothing boy; he will spoil everything again." The contrast between Francis and Metternich, who are usually lumped together as foes of freedom, is apparent in instance after instance: whether in the matter of reform in Austria or self-rule in Italy or censorship or the emperor's police-spies. This distinction between conservative and reactionary is not a mere quibble to whitewash Metternich or to score debating-points against liberals. Today the distinction is not only genuine but crucial. Too many Americans think they can oppose communism by backing not conservatives nor liberals but reactionaries like General Franco. Yet the backing of one such extreme only nourishes the growth of the other extreme —until this polarization ends the meaningful choice between freely voting conservative or freely voting liberal and forces a country into the meaningless Scylla-or-Charbydis choice of being enslaved by reactionary or radical terrorists.

After the death of Francis in 1835, his "retarded child" Ferdinand left the job of governing to a loose coalition of archdukes and ministers. Notable among the latter were the Czech finance-expert Kolowrat and, of course, Metternich himself. It was hard for the coalition to agree on the simplest steps, and Metternich and Kolowrat were open enemies; the latter was to plot the fall of the former behind the scenes of 1848. Such conditions paralyzed the top levels of administration, making reforms almost impossible and making stagnancy and stalemate the norm. Francis, being a stubborn fool, had at least given his country a unity of command impossible under the feeble fool who followed. The one clear gain for Austria, when Francis joined his anointed ancestors, was the relaxation of censorship, the increased practice of civil liberties. These pre-Revolution conditions of the 1830's and 1840's have been summarized as follows:

Publications within Austria were still subjected to a strict censorship, but Liberal pamphlets, newspapers, etc., were freely introduced from abroad. University professors were (in fact) allowed considerable latitude. Western European Liberal ideas rapidly took root among the educated classes of Austria. In Austria proper these ideas found expression in agitation for constitutional changes. . . . The movement for constitutional reform was stimulated by the industrial progress of Austria, giving Vienna and other cities an increasingly large middle class, cultivated, self-confident, eager to take its place in the political life of the country. Industry also brought a city proletariat with more radical views. . . . This was the setting for the events of March, 1848.[16]

For Metternich the monarchy, even a reformed and constitutional one, must remain the center of authority. It was a needed symbol of unity for the diverse Hapsburg nationalities, just as the British monarchy today is needed as the most vivid symbol of unity for the scattered British commonwealth. Even the Czech nationalist Palacky conceded that, if there were no Hapsburg monarchy, it would be necessary to invent it. The alternative was the chaotic Balkanization of the Danube union in 1919. By centralizing and Germanizing, Joseph II had offended the non-German nationalities and had almost caused a successful revolution. Decentralization, increased home rule, respect for local languages, respect for local constitutions, such were the measures needed to keep the non-Germans satisfied with Hapsburg rule. And such were the measures Metternich advocated in both Hungary and Italy.

His brakes on German aggression and on chauvinists like Jahn and Arndt were also in the interest of the Slavs, ever Germany's first victims. For them the conservative Metternich system turned out to be less oppressive than were the liberals who overthrew him. Evidence is the attitude of Palacky, leading the Pan-Slav Congress at Prague. His letter of April 11, 1848, rebuffing the Germanizing Frankfort liberals, put forward the Hapsburg empire as a buffer to save the non-Russian westernized Slavs from both Russian and German imperialism.

This solution might have unified the economy and politics of central and eastern Europe, blocking both Pan-Germanism and Russia's brand of Pan-Slavism. The solution required not the Austro-Hungarian dualism of 1867 but a Slav-Austro-Hungarian trialism, such as Archduke Franz Ferdinand would apparently have introduced on his succession to the throne. Was it too late, or would it have saved the Hapsburgs and the cause of Danubian unity? The bullets at Sarajevo in 1914 prevent us from knowing the answer.

Typical of Metternich's middleway position is a letter he wrote to Gentz from Hungary:

> Certainly a democracy does not exist here; the struggle goes on between the pure Royalists and the friends of constitution. Since the Emperor Joseph II's accession to the throne, the Government opposed the Constitution. I caused the Emperor to take a reversed position within the bounds of the Constitution.[17]

Metternich here was a "friend of constitution;" that is, a friend of lawful rule based on consent. He was no friend of the lawless dictatorship of pure Royalists. Neither was he a friend of democracy. Though England might be ready for it, he never considered uneducated and politically backward cultures to be ready for political activism. Perhaps this attitude is too patronizing, the superciliousness of an Anglophile snob. Or perhaps it is history-minded realism, aware of the centuries of evolution and of the most slow and cautious extensions of the franchise which alone made democracy workable in England, "the freest land" (as Metternich said) "because the best disciplined."[18]

Equally typical of Metternichian conservatism is his comment on the liberal revolution in Naples: "A people who can neither read nor write, whose last word is the dagger—such a people offers fine material for constitutional principles!"[19] But in Italy, as in Austria, Metternich tried to combine reforms for the people as a whole to balance his repressions against the tiny revolutionary minority. When a people is unfit for democracy because it "can neither read nor write," only the reactionaries would want to keep it that way. Vainly the Austrian Foreign Minister asked Francis I to facilitate Italian "educational arrangements." Here, too, history books damn the Minister for his ruler's hate of reforms.

Francis's solution for Italian grievances was further repression. Metternich's solution in 1817, which might have prevented the revolts of the 1820's and of 1848, was to remove the grievances. His letter of November 3, 1817 to his Emperor supports our hypothesis that Metternich would have fulfilled the three new forces of the age by assimilating them with the old forces. The more feasible demands of democracy and the more justified demands of capitalism and nationality, all three mutually conflicting, he would have harmonized through proportion and moderation. Consistent with the motto "Force within Law," he would have fulfilled them conservatively; that is, *within* the lawful framework of the old empire. Under almost any other monarch, he might have succeeded.

His letter of 1817 first of all outlines for Francis "the main causes to which this discontent is ascribed." These are: "the tedious progress of business, the design attributed to your Majesty of wishing to give an entirely German character to the Italian provinces, the composition of the courts, where the Italians daily see with sorrow German magistrates appointed to offices." Then follow some of Metternich's interesting remedies, showing his awareness of the new force of middle-class capitalism ("the progress of business") as well as of democratic liberalism ("a constitution") and nationality ("conciliate the national spirit"):

> I think it my duty to repeat again, with the greatest respect, how important it would be, from a political point of view, to remove as soon as possible these defects and shortcomings in the most interesting part of the monarchy, to quicken and advance the progress of business, to conciliate the national spirit and self-love of the nation by giving to these provinces a form of *constitution*, which might prove to the Italians that we have no desire to deal with them as with the German provinces of the monarchy, or, so

to speak, to weld them with these provinces; that we should there appoint, especially in the magisterial offices, able natives of the country.[20]

What was the monarch's reaction to such reforms, which his minister wanted "as soon as possible"? The ensuing drama of Francis is, as we shall see, tragically hilarious and helps explain why the Hapsburg empire is no longer with us.

Apart from the Italian reforms, Metternich in 1817 also urged freer institutions for the empire as a whole, with an embryonic parliament which, once started, would inevitably have assumed an ever greater governing power. Central Europe might have followed England's evolutionary road to self-government instead of the static stagnation that bred rapid revolution. His plans (to summarize from two different memoranda of that year) included "a deliberative body of notables," partly elected by provincial diets and partly appointed, to represent the country in "scrutiny of the budget and every law." Interesting, in view of the national tensions that later wrecked the Danube empire, is his plan of separate constitutions and separate chancellors for the national minorities, protecting them from the oppression of Germanization ("an Italian chancellor over Lombardy and Venetia;" another one for the Czechs and Poles of Bohemia, Moravia, and Galicia; one for German Austria proper; and still another for the largely Yugoslav province then known as "Illyria").[21]

And the result? Nine years later, after a serious illness, Francis said to Metternich: "Do you know what tormented me most when I expected to die? It was the thought of having left lingering on my table your report of 1817. But now, without losing a day more, I shall lay hold of the Council of State with it." On the royal table, the memorandum (it was one of the two dealing with a parliament) continued to "linger" dustily. After another nine years, in 1835, Francis—whose famous motto for solving all questions was "let's sleep on it" —promised Metternich, "Before the end of the year this question [of the 1817 report] will be solved." Two months later he was dead.[22]

Even earlier than 1817, there had been Metternich's demand of 1809 for modernizing Austria and his unheeded reform-plans of 1811. As late as 1847, he vainly urged the archdukes to increase the constitutional rights of the provinces. (Ironically too late, just before his fall in 1848, he was at last winning acceptance of his ancient plan of convoking delegates from all the provincial estates to a representative body in Vienna, but the revolution struck first.) In short, no matter how often he "repeated again, with the greatest respect"—when it came to reform, he was strait-jacketed.

Was any more feasible reform-program than Metternich's offered by the revolutionists who overthrew him? Not if we accept at least some of the lessons he deduced from the French Revolution, in which he had witnessed the consequences of giving the people rapidly instead of gradually a sovereignty for which they were not yet trained. He felt that the liberals who wanted this, and not he, were freedom's enemies. In this he was to some extent correct, as shown by the miserable end of all the liberal revolutions of 1848. Almost every nation participating in '48 found itself more despotically governed afterwards than before. The Hungarians lost the constitution that Metternich had restored to them; the French got the dictatorship of Napoleon III; the Prussians got their Iron Chancellor; and the Germans got Prussia.

If Metternich refused to turn over the government to those "who could neither read nor write," he built for their future by his untiring encouragement of education. In his defense of Europe against the aggressive nationalism of the Jahns and Arndts, he did, it is true, inexcusably suspend academic freedom in the German universities. With this important black exception, the plain facts refute the assumption of our textbooks that he was an obscurantist persecuting the world of learning. He was the friend and financial sponsor of leading educators of his day. We find him fostering art academies in Vienna, Milan, Venice, Rome. At the same time he served the material needs of his people, so that we also find him busily founding high schools *(Realschulen)*, polytechnical institutes, industrial exhibitions, and public endowments to encourage new inventions and to import foreign industrial experts. His introduction of a railroad system did much to spread ideas as well as economic goods.[23]

The crimes of the Austrian censorship can now be traced chiefly to the Police President, the unbelievable Sedlnitzky. The police spies were the darlings of their protector, Emperor Francis, whose joy was the daily perusal of intercepted private mail. Liberals persist in blaming Metternich for not ordering a halt to police persecutions in Vienna—Metternich, who vainly ordered the police to stop opening the mail of his closest collaborator Gentz. The latter was finally forced to use secret messengers for his correspondence with Metternich![24]

Such was the "charming" atmosphere of old Vienna. In the context of Sedlnitzky and Francis, there is an aura of pathos about Metternich's foredoomed ambition "to give Vienna the intellectual importance enjoyed by Paris." Yet he continued, undismayed, to bring scholars and educators to Vienna and to finance and direct journals dedicated, like the *Jahrbücher* of 1817, to the spread of knowledge and critical thinking among the Austrian peoples. Important in Austrian intellectual history is the "Imperial Academy of Sciences," founded under his direction, perhaps in imitation of the French Academy. He adopted the principle "that the freedom of its utterances in speech and writing suffer no restrictions except that of its own self-censorship *(Selbstzensur)*." As usual, he was soon overruled by his colleagues and by Sedlnitzky on this issue of academic freedom for his "Academy."[25] In view of such domestic obstacles, in view of the pressing call of his foreign diplomatic duties, and in view of his reputation as a pleasure-loving idler, the amount and diversity of his work for education is all the more impressive.

Earlier than Karl Marx, Metternich was among the first to point out a fact of increasing interest today: namely, that the liberty for which the capitalist fought was sometimes a means to substitute an economic oligarchy for the existing political aristocracy. Amid the clamor for and against representative institutions, he calmly explained that these would in practice become an instrument not of the people but of the business class. Unlike the situation in the commercialized America of today, where we are all equally middle class from workers to millionaires, the European middle class was then still a minority pressure-group, totally unrepresentative of the "people" it claimed to represent. "The first instrument in the hands of the middle class is the modern representative system" (not Marx but Metternich speaking!), "this caricature of the English constitution because it has none of the fundamental conditions whereby it could attain to its model."[26] These were Metternich's words in 1831; and he went on to predict correctly that the next French revolution would be not middle class, as in 1830, but proletarian.

This reminds us again of his perceptive epigram: "What is called a constitution today is nothing but 'get out so that I can get in.' " His century's enthusiasm for that sort of constitution, Metternich was too sharp-eyed to share. No wonder most history books, still steeped in a middle-class version of liberalism, labeled this independent-minded aristocrat a hopeless reactionary.

Metternich was too good a monarchist and too good a "socialist" to believe a country was free if its individuals had unlimited freedom, which each could use to destroy the freedom of his poorer neighbors. The just state must limit such freedom by law (as America learnt after the depression of 1929); and it must be a nonarbitrary, nondespotic system of law, consecrated by tradition and enforced by objective legitimate authority. But authority purely in the political realm is not enough protection for the people. No longer politics but the "social problem" is what now counts, he wrote to Count Rechberg.[27] And in 1849, when the middle class was overthrowing monarchy and aristocracy all over Europe, Metternich added, "I shall die as I have lived, not as a politician but as a socialist."[28] This does not contradict his conservative philosophy. To express the unity of both his ideals he coined the phrase "conservative socialist" (*"socialiste conservateur"*). While still in power, he wrote to Premier Guizot:

The true character of our time is that of an era of *transition*. Fate imposed on me the duty of coming between the phases of this era. . . . To me the political game did not at all seem to answer to the needs of the time; I made myself a conservative socialist. The conservative principles are applicable to the most diverse situations; their worship is not enclosed within narrow bounds; they are enemies of anarchy, moral and material.[29]

Obviously we can hardly call him, the anti-materialist and distruster of the masses, a socialist in the modern Marxist sense of the word. "To ruin those who possess something," in his unradical opinion, "is not to come to the aid of those who possess nothing; it is only to render misery general."[30] Even less has his "conservative socialism" in common with Hitler's terroristic "National Socialism"; fascism, no matter what its disguise, incarnates that "moral anarchy" of which conservative principles are "enemies."

Metternich's key word, so prominent on his coat of arms, was always the word "law." What he meant by his "socialism" was simply that the rule of law, moral and economic in scope, must restrain the new middle-class seizers of power and must subordinate their capitalism to the common welfare. Their slogans of liberalism, progress, and antifeudalism he regarded as masks for exploitation and bourgeois dictatorship. In his day, the reality behind these masks was the misery of the industrial revolution, its slums and child labor and wretched working conditions, such as Marx was to describe in *Das Kapital* from an anti-Metternichian as well as anticapitalist viewpoint. Europe might have been spared these sufferings if the industrial revolution had, through control from above, been an industrial evolution, just as a political evolution avoids the bloodshed of a political revolution.

Both Metternich and Burke would have approved that Fabian Socialist phrase, "the inevitability of gradualness." In 1815, gradualism meant putting government brakes on the middle-class rush to power. It did not mean crushing the middle class (Metternich actively fostered its trade). But it means that monarchy and aristocracy and the state must not surrender to big money and big business in the fashion of the "bourgeois monarchy" of Louis Philippe.

We have already noted Metternich's gloating prediction that his middle-class foes of 1830 would, in turn, be ousted from below by the next revolution. His "secret thought" was that his class and theirs would both be swept away. Perhaps this is another reason why he liked the then-hated word "socialist." To the Russian diplomat Nesselrode, he made an amazing admission:

"I am always considered the rock of order, the obstacle to revolution and warlike enterprise, but I confess to you that my innermost and secret thought is that old Europe and its form of government are doomed; that between the old order and the new order to come will be a long period of chaos."[30a]

These are the sentiments and presentiments he may have felt, but dared not say, each time his sovereign vetoed such farsighted reforms as Metternich urged for Italy in 1817 and for Austria in 1832. Another such "secret thought" occurs in a letter Metternich wrote from Vienna on October 6, 1820:

"My life has fallen at a hateful time. I have come into the world either too early or too late. Now I do not feel comfortable; earlier, I should have enjoyed the time; later I should have helped to build it up again; today I have to give my life to prop up the moldering edifice."[31]

This comment on the moldering social system of monarchs like Francis recalls the protest of Hamlet:

> The world is out of joint. O cursèd spite,
> That ever I was born to set it right,

and the nostalgia of Matthew Arnold:

> Wandering between two worlds, one dead,
> The other powerless to be born.

Certainly these private doubts of a tired 18th-century gentleman contradict his self-confident public announcements. And they contradict the last words he ever spoke—he was 86, and this was 1859—to his friend Hübner: "I have been a rock of order;" then a pause; then, turning away, changing from

German to French, and mumbling as if only to himself: *"un rocher d'ordre."*[32] Some two weeks later, the octogenarian lingerer in an evolving world died, just when the Hapsburg troops were being ousted in the Italian war and while Darwin was publishing his book on evolution.

In view of the contradiction between his "secret thoughts" and his pose of *un rocher*, he must have been more complex than his biographers have fathomed. In his impressionable youth, he had perhaps suffered a psychological trauma when he saw his secure Rhineland home overrun by the French Revolution, which suddenly made him an insecure refugee. Ever after: an ambivalence between the insecurity of imminent revolution and the need to reassure himself by playing the role of the "never-shattered rock in the waves of chaos." In concepts like "conservative socialist" or "stability is not immobility," he tried to bridge both sides of the ambivalence. This is the task which the evolutionary conservative is forever attempting (Pericles, Cicero, Erasmus, Burke, Loris-Melikov, Disraeli, Stolypin, Churchill) and which the static reactionary ever refuses.

Metternich as rock: though privately a façade for his inner doubts, this rôle met the emotional needs of a repose-craving[33] and revolution-shocked generation. Compare the post-1815 revival of the church, the oldest rock of all. Hence, the general European acceptance of the Metternich system in 1815. It must have ruled by popular consent far more than is now believed, for the fact is that it had surprisingly few troops or weapons at its disposal. The Revolution of 1848 was the work of a new generation with new psychological needs, a generation which had not experienced the horrors of war and revolution and whose middle class was as eager to seize power from the landed gentry as the Parisian proletariat was to seize it from the middle class.

To Metternich the French Revolution was "the volcano which must be extinguished, the gangrene which must be burnt out with the hot iron, the hydra with jaws open to swallow the social order." Such crudely lurid metaphors may be contrasted with Wordsworth's early reaction to the very same Revolution:

Bliss was it in that dawn tc be alive
But to be young was very heaven.

One would hardly think both men were gazing at the same
occurrence. Yet both their descriptions are valid. One saw
the ideals and the other the practice, one the ends and the
other the corrupting means to the ends. The same contrast in
emotional responses is daily evoked by any mention of the
Russian Revolution.

Could this early shock have given Metternich a compulsive
phobia about all later revolutionary movements, even the
harmless bumptiousness of student-chatter? At times he seemed
to fear the milder French revolutionists of the 1830's as if
they were still the regicides of 1793. Burke, too, could find no
metaphors too lurid for the French Revolution. Yet Burke
admired the American Revolution (would not a more accurate
name be "the American Conservation"?). And this with consistency, for 1776 conserved the established traditional liberties
of freeborn Englishmen, as already confirmed in 1688. Against
these traditions, it is the innovating usurpations of George III
—against both America and the English parliament—that
were the real "Revolution of 1776."

In addition to the psychological distortions in his political
philosophy, Metternich's efficacy suffered from shortcomings
of personality even when his politics was at its most enlightened. These shortcomings appeared each time Francis rejected
Metternich's suggestions for the reforms that might have
averted 1848. Instead of either resigning honorably (say, in
1832) or insisting on his way, either turning his back or pound-
ing on the table, he shrugged his shoulders and consoled himself
with his amusing salons and mistresses. (Of the latter, according to the indignant Treitschke, he adorned his gracious existence with never less than two at a time.) He was a grand
seigneur, not a fighter.[34] And he succumbed at times to the
famous Viennese *Schlamperei,* that euphoric state of self-
satisfied muddling. In this he was soothed by his vanity.[35]
Prince Metternich sometimes betrayed Professor Metternich.
One can only conclude that the modern conservative must

avert his own 1848 by fighting as vigorously and sincerely for the positive and social-reformist half of his program as for the negative and defensive half.

Francis crushed his minister's reform projects but egged on his repressions. Believing that the Marats and Robespierres of his youth had killed freedom in the name of freedom, Metternich refused to concede that freedom included unbridled agitation for demagogues and violent revolutionists. Yet one man's demagogue is another man's statesman. "Violent revolution," even when a "clear and present danger" (to use 1949 terminology), is hard to define legally without passing legislation that tyrants can later use against the innocent.

On the other hand, the fifth-column danger to freedom today is not necessarily a "red herring" or "witch hunt," as the Czech democracy learnt twice in one decade. The following question must be debated with an open mind rather than oversimplified or answered dogmatically: will any given measure our democracy passes against conspiracy endanger civil liberties less or more than do the conspirators? Neither Metternich's age nor ours has solved this worrisome dilemma. Yet the very fact that such a dilemma can exist and can worry us is a consoling proof that our freedom still exists also. In eastern Europe it would not be a dilemma in the first place, and the inability to comprehend western qualms would be sincere.

"Nothing is so free as a man's thought," wrote Metternich at the height of his Carlsbad censorship program. Was this hypocrisy, or did he use the expression in a special sense when he added that "free thought" helped "give life its greatest value"?[36] In futile protest against his Emperor's intolerance, Metternich once warned, "It is useless to close the gates against ideas; they overleap them all the same and arrive by contraband."[37] This stricture can be neatly turned against Metternich himself as author of censorship imposed on Germany after 1819.

Yet his aim was not to curtail *free* thought but to curtail the enslavement of free *thought* by irrational *emotions*. Made today, such a distinction would be an insincere sophistry for the purpose of undermining civil liberties. But the distinction was, or seemed, more than theoretical hair-splitting in the context of 1819. The emotional and unthoughtful "free thought" of some nationalists and antimonarchist leftists included the following: several little "liberal" conspiracies for violent revolt and assassination; the unliberal racism that made Heine fear a pogrom; the proto-Nazism of influential demagogues like Jahn; the terrorism and political murder preached to students by the Jena "unconditional" faction, to which belonged Kotzebue's murderer Sand, soon hailed as national hero by fanatics who dipped their daggers in his blood. These German groups were more dangerous than realized by most historians.

Yet these Germans, though influential, were a small minority as yet. Their presence called for urgent specialized action against murder and lawlessness but not for general action against lawful liberalism. Metternich claimed they necessitated his Carlsbad Decrees for censoring German writing and teaching as a whole. He was wrong. Carlsbad was Metternich at his frequent unconservative worst, reactionary and anticonstitutional.

The Carlsbad spirit was not the whim of one man, one government, or one country. It expressed the mood of a generation which only four years ago was still being drenched with blood by the armies of the Revolution and which now wanted and needed (as Metternich rightly said) "repose." That you can get repose by suppression and that all radical movements are bloodthirsty because Marat was bloodthirsty, these are certainly illusions. But they were illusions endemic in all countries that had suffered from the Jacobin wars and are not specifically Metternichian, conservative, or Austrian. England is often thought of as the liberal white, juxtaposed to Metternich's repressive black. Yet in that same year 1819, the lawfully elected British government suspended *habeas corpus,* fired on English crowds at Peterloo, and passed the repressive Six Acts. No German nor Austrian crowds were fired on during the Carlsbad equivalent of the Six Acts. And in England there was far less danger to civilization to justify repression. There were no proto-Nazi nationalists. Instead, there were the genuinely democratic liberals whose civilized values, as later expressed in Chartism, have now been accepted as strengthening a free society.

We can best realize how Europe has changed when we recall that liberals and radicals were not executed in 1819; this would have been as unthinkable as sentencing political offenders to slave labor. Even the worst mistakes and repressions under Francis were *still within the framework of civilization.* This must be contrasted with the millions executed and enslaved by a Hitler or Stalin, now that the conservative internationalists have been replaced by their nationalist or communist foes. Bad enough, and a loss for Germany, that the annoying pinpricks of censorship made brilliant liberals like Heine move to Paris. And bad enough that Nicholas I, the cruelest despot of his century, sentenced his liberal critic Polizhaev to serve as a common soldier, "clearing your name in the army," while kissing him on the forehead for the imagined necessity of such sternness. In our own progressive century, unburdened by such Hapsburg and Romanov aristocrats, a plebeian Hitler or Stalin simply signs his name and the tight-packed trucks shift gears and speed off to the gas chambers or the firing squads.

Future historians will see the national socialism of Hitler and the national bolshevism of Stalin as variations on a single historical theme: the totalitarian mass-man. Both variations trumpet the word "socialism" for demagogic reasons and because it sounds so folksy. But both begin by abolishing the right to strike and end by turning their workers into slave labor. The ruling class is an oligarchy (not the same as aristocracy— the distinction is Plato's) of bureaucrats and police. How soon will the oligarchy become hereditary? Perhaps dialectics can prove that all men are born equal but some more equal than others. The difference in economic standard of living and in political rights between a typical Soviet slave-laborer and a commissar is many times greater than between the poorest American worker and an American millionaire. Slave labor, between seven and fifteen millions and under deadliest working conditions, has apparently become the most typical institution of the Soviet Union's Stalinist phase.[38]

For a 19th-century prophecy of this fascist-bolshevist synthesis, read not Marx but Konstantin Leontyev, that curious prophet who was among the first to foresee Stalinism and to name its causes. While the historian Hans Kohn interprets Leontyev's description of this phenomenon as mainly enthusiastic, the philosopher Berdyaev interprets it as ironic, written out of bitter despair. Perhaps such ambiguities can arise because Leontyev, like many other sincere opponents of tsarist expansionism, could not help being also influenced by the Moscow "Third Rome" tradition of his milieu. Even an anarchist like Bakunin was sufficiently steeped in this history-molding tradition (Moscow as heir of the two earlier world-capitals, Rome and Constantinople) to proclaim: "It will be in Moscow that the star of the Revolution will rise, out of an ocean of blood and fire, and will become the guiding star of all humanity." In his famous book *1984,* published in 1949, George Orwell concludes with the revolutionist's breakdown before total authority: "He *loved* Big Brother." This mentality is a leitmotif not only of modern totalitarianism but also of Russian history since Ivan the Terrible. The rebel's breakdown before the Big Brother symbol of absolute power was anticipated in real life by a letter of Bakunin. In 1851 the prison-chastened anarchist wrote of his own accord to Nicholas I, "In spite of my democratic convictions, I have worshipped you profoundly in the last years, as it were against my will. . . . Russia needs a strong dictatorial power . . . not limited by anybody or anything."

As terrifying as *1984*—Leontyev's preview of Orwell might have been called *1917*—is Leontyev's letter of 1890, explaining the dual appeal, autocratic and revolutionary, of what today may be called "Red tsarism":

Sometimes I see a *Russian tsar at the head of the Russian movement of revolutionary Socialism,* organizing it as Emperor Constantine organized Christianity. But what does such organization mean? Nothing else than constraint, an enlightened despotism, the legitimization of a chronic violence, applied in adroit and wise doses, a violence which exercises itself upon the personal will of the citizens. It is hardly probable that one could organize this new and rather complex slavery and make it last without a mystic faith. If after Russia's annexation of Constantinople an extraordinary concentration of the Orthodox ecclesiastical bureaucracy should coincide with the development of the mystic faith, and with the inevitable *workers' movement,* one could guarantee for a long time the political and economic bases of the state.

Seeing this tsarist communism as reactionary and radical at the same time, Leontyev added: "Only a strong monarchical authority, limited solely by its conscience and sanctified by faith, can solve the contemporary problem which seems to us insoluble—the conciliation of capital and labor. We must draw ahead of Europe on the question of labor, and we must set the example." Why must the authority of this labor monarch exclude civil liberties for his liberated subjects? "Our people love and understand authority better than law. They consider a military chief more accessible and even more sympathetic than an article of a legal code. A constitution which would weaken authority in Russia, would not have the time to inculcate the devotion the English have for legislation. . . . Our people need affirmative faith and material security more than they need rights and true science." As the climax of this "economic democracy" of the future, Leontyev predicted that "a new kind of slavery will emerge. It will probably adopt the cruelest form of domination the community could impose upon the individual and the state upon the community."[39]

Though still in transition, Stalinist Russia appears to be substituting what her press calls "proletarian nationalism" for the internationalism of Marx and Engels. Or, rather, not so much substituting as welding both together, resolving the contradiction by a return to the tsarist paranoia of a Russian national mission to save the world, saving it this time for the only orthodox socialist religion instead of the only orthodox Christian religion. This is the development Engels feared and foresaw in a letter warning against many of his 19th-century Russian socialists "who still believe in an elementary Communist mission of holy Russia, unlike the other nations of 'infidels.' "[40]

This holy national mission was founded in the 16th century by Ivan the Terrible, who called Moscow the "Third Rome," the "New Jerusalem," the only "Noah's Ark" for a drowning world. Founder of a nation-wide secret police, eloquent preacher of absolute dictatorship, and recognized as one of the cruelest mass-murderers in world history, Ivan the Terrible is glorified in the Soviet People's Democracy as a People's Tsar and as the forerunner of Joseph I. Americans will recall the Soviet cinema about Ivan; no westerner can afford to miss it, not for its inaccurate picture of the 16th century but for its accurate picture of contemporary Russian attitudes.[41] Probably the most perceptive essay ever written on Soviet realities is *Russia and Freedom* by the scholarly historian George Fedotov, who concludes:

> The new Soviet man is not so much modelled in the Marxist school as he crept into the light out of [Ivan the Terrible's] Muscovite tsardom, slightly glossed over with Marxism. . . . The Soviet man is more akin to the [16th-century] Muscovite through his proud national consciousness: his country is the only Orthodox, the only Socialist, the first country in the world, the "Third Rome." He does not know the west, dislikes it and fears it. And as of old his soul is open to the east. . . . Coming together with foreigners, the Russians of the Empire had to blush for their autocracy and slavery. Had they everywhere met obsequiousness to the Russian Tsar similar to that now shown by some Europeans and Americans for Stalin, it would never have occurred to them that something was wrong in their own home. The adulators of Stalin and of Soviet Russia are now the main enemies of Russian freedom.[42]

An example of this "new Soviet man" shedding his thin Marxist "gloss" is the 1949 drive against that supreme crime, "cosmopolitanism" and "subversive" internationalism. This drive is not only in the obvious field of politics. It is active in the great music purge.[43] It is active inside the Union of Soviet Writers, which in March, 1949 expelled writers guilty of being "antipatriot" and "cosmopolitan." "Cosmopolitanism," classified as a "subversive activity," was characterized by the spokesman of the writers' union, as a "desire to undermine," indirectly facilitating "American imperialism" by undermining "national roots and national pride."[44]

The same Soviet shedding of Marxist gloss is active in science. Here foreign devils have already been exorcized from biology and heredity by official action of the Communist Party in the Lysenko case.[45] In 1949, typically and still more recently, M. Mitin, an important member of the Soviet Academy of Sciences, denounced "an abstract world science which allegedly knows no national and state boundaries." He demanded the purge of Professor Boris Kedrov, a leading scholar and editor of a learned periodical, for having made in the past "such monstrous assertions" as that "science might be international." Such an attitude, explained Mitin, is subversive, being guilty of "discarding everything national and self-sufficient in the development of Russian social thought."[46] At a Soviet meeting Kedrov's dismissal from the faculty of the Institute of Philosophy was demanded on these grounds. Only a fortnight later, perhaps feeling on his neck a persuasive breeze from Siberia, Professor Kedrov hastened to confess his heresy publicly:

> I consider it my party duty to state that I fully agree with this criticism, and definitely denounce the advocacy of alien cosmopolitan viewpoints which I permitted myself to pursue. . . . Any mistake of a cosmopolitan character is not only theoretical but political, inasmuch as it inflicts direct harm on the cause of educating our people in Soviet patriotism. Of such character were the mistakes I made.[47]

The book and music purge, or the case of Lysenko or of Mitin and Kedrov, are not isolated but typical. The whole thing seems a Kremlin resurrection of Hitler, with Russian biology, art, music opposing the ideal of objective truth and international culture in much the same way as once did Aryan biology, art, music and so on.

The Hitler-Stalin police-state breaks more radically than Marxism with the traditional ethical order of the west. Marxism is invalidated by its 19th-century fad of economic determinism, which falsifies history and psychology. But in contrast with the nationalist police-state, Marxism has at least three points in its favor. It is international. Its ultimate aim, even though unattainable by its class-war methods, is brotherhood instead of war and slavery. And it does not revolt against reason but conserves much of the western rational tradition. These three points are even more true of the peaceful, parliamentary, non-Marxist socialists of England and Scandinavia.

Antisocialist monomaniacs in America may soon be hailing a suddenly avuncular "Joe" Stalin for his "common sense" in not practicing Marxist "radicalism." (Already in 1939, this attitude was decisive in Stalin's ally Hitler, who had "great admiration for Stalin" and "was only afraid some radical might come in his place.")[48] America's right-wing isolationist appeasers and opponents of the Atlantic pact should recall, as a recent war might have taught us, that there is a graver threat than socialism to individual liberty, and its name is fascism. Therefore, they must not imagine that Russia's gradual abandonment of Marxism reduces her threat. On the contrary, her slave-labor society, with its unappeasable fascist-style nationalism, is not a movement "back to common sense" but a movement from bad to worst of all.

In September, 1947 at a conference of Communist Party representatives, the late Zhdanov, director of the Cominform and second to Stalin, made an official speech putting Russia on record as the champion of "national sovereignty." Using as pretext Hitler's old allegation that collective security masks Yankee imperialism, Zhdanov denounced that growing international unity which alone can guard peace against the nationalist aggressor:

> One of the lines taken by the ideological campaign that goes hand in hand with the plans for the enslavement of Europe is an attack on the principles of national sovereignty, an appeal for the renouncement of the sovereign rights of nations, to which is opposed the idea of a "world government." . . . *The idea of a "world government" has been taken up by bourgeois intellectual cranks and pacifists* . . . against the Soviet Union, which indefatigably upholds the principle of real equality and protection of the sovereign rights of all nations, big and small.[49]

These sentiments were echoed at the "Cultural and Scientific Conference for World Peace" called in New York, March 1949. Here Alexander A. Fadeyev, head of the Russian delegation, secretary general of the Union of Soviet Writers, and a leader of the 1949 Soviet cultural drive against Jews[50] and cosmopolitans, proclaimed the official Communist stand on the Atlantic pact: "We Soviet intellectuals can only see in such pacts an attempted attack on the national sovereignty of peoples, the disruption of their national cultures . . ."[51]

In the opinion of this particular "bourgeois intellectual crank," what ails Europe is that there is no Europe. Since 1848, there have been only what Zhdanov, Fadeyev, and the rest call "national sovereignties." Once long ago, on the tinier city-state level, this clinging to warring local sovereignties wrecked the greatest civilization of all time. Now that weapons are more lethal than Hellenic spears, there may be no third chance if we cling to the wrong choice again. Hence, the Atlantic pact and the council of Europe. The task of 1949 is to undo 1848 through an internationalism strong enough to outlaw war by protecting the free and "quarantining the aggressor."

Today as in Metternich's day, the only sane asylum in a world of insane nationalism is an internationalism based on the middle way of balance and moderation. This rules out an internationalism based on extremes of left or right. Metternich warned against monarchist as well as revolutionary agitators of mob emotion because both produced what he deemed society's greatest danger: fanaticism. He feared not only the French Revolution's attack on religion but the anti-rational religious reaction that followed 1815: "The human mind generally revels in extremes. A period of irreligion . . . has been necessarily followed by . . . religious reaction. Now, every kind of reaction is false and unjust."[52] In one sentence he characterized the extremist pendulum-swings of Tsar Alexander: "In 1815 he abandoned pure Jacobinism but only to throw himself into mysticism."[53]

To Gentz, who likewise distrusted leftist and rightist fanaticism, Metternich summed up: "My constant efforts are directed against ultras of all kinds."[54] And in 1825: "The red and white doctrinaires shun me like the plague."[55] It is psychologically interesting that Metternich's boyhood tutor, of whom he always remained fond, was the *philosophe* Simon, who did not conceal his enthusiasm for the French Revolution and who—like the tutor of Alexander I—left to become a prominent Jacobin. Perhaps influenced by his tutor but never converted, Metternich said of his own early youth: "From the school of radicalism I fell into that of the émigrés and learned to value the mean between the extremes."[56] Of the extreme Royalists of the French Restoration, who rallied round Charles X, Metternich said: "The Legitimists are legitimatizing the Revolution."[57] In 1834 he coined the happy phrase "White Radicals" for them.[58]

Like "conservative socialist," the phrase "White Radicals" seems contradictory. But it means that the radical as well as "the conservative principles are applicable to the most diverse situations." Shortly before the Revolution of 1830, he had warned Charles X against those reactionary excesses which were to provoke the overthrow of France's last Bourbon king. Metternich considered Charles's unconstitutional ultraroyalist July Ordinances "of a nature not to solve but to cut through the matters and questions in dispute."[59]

To his confidante, Countess Darja Lieven, Metternich wrote: "You believe I am a liberal in the bottom of my heart? Yes, my friend. I am and even beyond it."[60] If his words were sincere and not a flirtatious jest, he could only have meant that he sought the same free and peaceful goal as the western liberals. But a liberal he was certainly not, taking the word in the sense of the contemporary liberal revolts of the 1820's. He lacked their faith in the natural goodness of man and in the masses, their faith in abstract rootless constitutions, their faith in man's ability to change basically his own nature or to break with the inescapable past.

The key is his qualifying the statement of "I am a liberal" by adding "and even beyond it." "Even beyond" implies both his aristocratic conservatism and his prophetic "socialism;" and both of these, being antibourgeois from opposite directions, were beyond the comprehension of his enemies, the narrow and unimaginative "bourgeois liberals." (Not that liberals need be either narrow or bourgeois; in our own time and country, these pejorative adjectives apply at least as often to stuffy-stodgy conservatives as to liberals.)

In central Europe after 1848, first the rebels and then the *Realpolitik* militarists like Schwarzenberg and Bismarck cut short Metternich's conservative way to freedom. Yet it did live on successfully—not in his own country but in England, through the enlightened Toryism of his self-styled pupil Disraeli, who still called him "my dear master" after his fall. Among other things, Metternich suggested the title "Conservative" for Disraeli's new party, good advice which the latter followed, making Metternich's favorite political adjective famous to this day, whether loved or hated, throughout the English-speaking world. Metternich personally inspired Disraeli's sensational speech in which the latter attacked the liberal Palmerston for his support on the Continent of "this modern, newfangled, sentimental principle of nationality."[61] According to Disraeli's biographers, "The following passage in [Disraeli's book] *Lord George Bentinck* would have been adopted by Metternich, even if it did not owe something to his inspiration:

"The European must be governed either by *traditionary influences or by military force.* Those who in their ardour of renovation imagine . . . our societies can be reconstructed on the great *Transatlantic model,* will find that, when they have destroyed traditionary influences, there will be peculiar features in their body politic which do not obtain in the social standard which they imitate, and these may be described as *elements of disturbance.* A dynasty may be subverted, but it leaves as its successor a family of princely pretenders; a confiscated aristocracy takes the shape of factions; a plundered Church acts on the tender consciences of toiling millions; corporate bodies displaced from their ancient authorities no longer contribute their necessary and customary quota to the means of government; *outraged tradition* in multiplied forms enfeebles or excruciates the reformed commonwealth.

"In this state of affairs, after a due course of paroxysms, for the sake of maintaining order and securing the rights of industry, the state quits the senate and takes refuge in the camp.

"Let us not be deluded by forms of government. . . . Irresistible law dooms Europe to the alternate sway of disciplined armies or secret societies; the camp or the convention."[62]

Like many of Metternich's own prophecies, this echo by his pupil did not become urgently clear until the 1938-1948 decade of world conquest by Hitler and Stalin. After World War I (to apply Disraeli's analysis) it was easy enough for the liberal victors to destroy the "traditionary influences" in the defeated monarchies. But this confident "renovating" attempt to reconstruct central Europe "on the great Transatlantic model," could not restore the sense of order it had destroyed. It drove industry and the state to "take refuge in the camp" —in fascism, in the terrorist police-state of a Hitler or Mussolini or Franco or Stalin. To sum up in Disraeli's own Victorian diction: the hasty liberal reformer, "outraging" the historical pattern of his society, has unintentionally "excruciated the commonwealth."

What worries the conservative is not so much the liberal as his grandson. The liberal himself is a benign and beamish soul, as well behaved as you could wish, for he is still living on the moral capital accumulated by past conservatives. Even when he most undermines it, he unknowingly lives on the security of this past capital. And so do his children. Until the atonement when the moral account is overdrawn. Here is a Europe-inspired fable in three chapters, condensed perhaps to the point of unfairness as caricatures are, a FABLE FOR AMERICANS:

· · · ·

Chapter One. Burning with innocent leftist enthusiasm, the liberal hacks away at what he calls aristocratic values. So far, so good. These often are exploited by reactionaries and do need revision. Meanwhile, no sign of barricades, no heads rolling in the sand—how this justifies his forward-looking enlightenment, how foolish the fears of the priggish conservatives! The liberal continues to be brought his cosy bourgeois breakfast and his progressive morning newspaper with soothing regularity, protected by the order he scorns. Unfortunately his weapon against the undemocratic values is not a moral democracy of Christian brotherhood but the two-edged sword of relativism: "All standards, morals, and traditions are relative, merely reflecting self-interest and economics." So it's hurrah for change, full speed ahead; and it's down with home and hearth, throne and altar, quaint honor and old loyalties—that noise was merely Chekhov's cherry orchard crashing—and everything banal and benighted. Again: so far, so good. Why not clear the house of what's "outdated"? Considered in isolation and out of historical context: yes, why not? Chapter One ends merrily, to the glorious music of bursting chains.

Chapter Two. Next comes the liberal's son. What a clever fellow! Brought up in daddy's emancipated milieu, this Wise Guy knows all the answers; he denies not merely aristocratic values now but—values. Are they not "all relative"? Have not psychology and semantics proved everything a sentimental, self-deceiving hoax? Everybody knows that everything is a gyp, an obvious racket. "Anything [to quote the typical title of a Broadway hit] Goes."

Chapter Three. The grandson is the real Realist. No Sunday-school manners in politics for him. None of poor soft grandpa's liberal qualms; none of father's cleverness either ("where does it get you?"); now it's tooth and claw in the struggle of egomaniac self-interests. And what faith he has, is in the state, all other faiths having been discredited. With no tradition of moral restraints to guide him and with the capital exhausted at last, the grandson shouts for a Hitler or a Stalin. And so, in three irresponsible generations, three thousand years of civilization perish to the music of radio lies and clanking chains, chains more efficient and cruel than ever the old ones. This in our lifetime—each of us who faced the Nazis, and now the Soviets, able to repeat, "I was the man, I suffered, I was there"—this; and artists complain they can no longer find "suitable subjects" for tragedy.

. . . .

All creeds claim to lead to freedom by their own patented routes. Some promise a quick and easy route at the price of liquidating the laws and ethical restraints that govern the material means we use. Metternich's way to freedom, like the way trod so successfully by free and conservative England, could only be achieved by a long, gradual education. On the Continent, this process was smashed in 1848, first by the fatal alliance of attractive liberal idealists with tough-guy nationalists and, second, by the resultant pendulum-swing to a sterile rightist despotism. Ever since, central and eastern Europe has alternated between unrepresentative extremes of right and left without establishing any really deep-rooted center—or what the French now call a "third force." This is the time Yeats foretold in his poem "The Second Coming," when

> Things fall apart; the centre cannot hold;
> Mere anarchy is loosed upon the world.
> The blood-dimmed tide is loosed. . . .
> The best lack all conviction, while the worst
> Are full of passionate intensity.[63]

It is difficult for youth or for the masses to feel "conviction" and "passionate intensity" about sober rational moderation. In other words, civilization is difficult. It is more romantic and intoxicating to shout "Not Christ but Barabbas" and to feel the mass-meeting enthusiasm generated by tyrants and revolutionists. That is why the concept of a central "third force" has always been, under different labels, a cultural and moral aspiration synonymous with civilization itself. Today this force, tormented by stupidity and treason but sustained by the vision and wisdom of the Marshall Plan, has ethical roots deeper than merely economic expedients and takes its stand in the ceaseless Armageddon of freedom. This may turn out to be the final stand of civil liberties and of the humane and tolerant sense of mutual concession on which they depend. Such a union today must embrace all forces of moderation, broad enough to include parliamentary socialists and parliamentary capitalists.

The delicate fabric of civilized values is strained to the breaking-point by the westward push of terror and totalitarianism, no matter whether this protean barbarism be a return to Nordic berserkers or to the Tartar knout of the steppes. When "Genghis Khan plus the telegraph" (this synthesis of medieval autocracy with modern technocracy) sweeps to the English Channel, that day will be not the decline but the fall of the west.

The wars, chaos, and centerless extremism of 1914-1949 are the logical outcome of the 1848 polarization of Europe. We are the last agonisants of the Metternichian tragedy. His conservation of a durable international order—his Europeanness—was frustrated in the end. It was weakened by his own misdeeds (the gap between Prince and Professor; his panicky Carlsbad spirit which it is not my purpose to whitewash) and was annihilated by two sets of extremists:

1. The feudal-minded rulers, whose kingdoms his diplomacy could save from Napoleon but not from themselves, were blind to his Burkean kind of conservatism, which would reconcile through free institutions "the monarchist principle and the democratic."

2. The rising capitalist middle class, agitating the masses it claimed to represent in '48, subordinated its original liberalism to nationalism. His cosmopolitan unity was confronted with the passionate insanities of national egotism and racism. Here he was really fighting the first germs of the Nazi epidemic: the Führer cult, anti-Semitism, and Pan-German expansionism proclaimed by such Metternich-hating "liberal heroes of '48" as Jahn and Wagner. Metternich, the last European, was the first man in Europe to foresee the German fascist menace when he charged that the nationalist hysteria in Prussia was not normal patriotic love of country but a new kind of Jacobin terror. In view of the World Wars, crematories, and concentration camps of modern nationalism, which his internationalism would have prevented, the standard rhetoric about "Metternich's despotism" rings hollow.

Upon the United States of America, upon the heirs of the American Conservation of 1776, falls the task of conserving the western heritage today. As Metternich defended the internationalism and gradualism of the west against the proto-Nazis of German nationalism, so we must now help Europe help itself against new Munich Pacts, against the Nazism that lives on in Russian national bolshevism.

Like Metternich we have made not only strategic mistakes. We, too, have made moral mistakes—whenever we have supported reactionary forces abroad instead of a coalition of free conservative and liberal forces. Coming later, we can learn better from these mistakes than he did; we can still correct them. Our cause, like his, is not white but gray. This makes it the more urgent for gray to redeem itself: externally, by defending the gray west against the black of the Soviets; internally, by expanding social reforms and civil liberties to prevent black reaction at home. Our cause, like his, is the cause of the second best against the worst; while the best exists only in an imaginary Rousseauistic society without a past and without political Original Sin.

When Metternich was driven into exile, Disraeli had written (far too gushingly yet sincerely): "You are the only philosophical statesman I ever encountered. . . . I catch wisdom from your lips and inspiration from your example."[64] After the Congress of Berlin, two decades after Metternich's death, seeing Europe ripped apart by nationalist hates, Disraeli exclaimed, "All Metternich's predictions took place; he had truly the gift of prophetic vision."[65] But is not vision usually appreciated too late? After 1848, the liberal Count Széchényi, who had unintentionally paved the way for the disastrous revolution in Hungary, bewailed his disregard of the great conservative's counsel:

"Prince Metternich always warned me that I was doing wrong. He told me: Do not touch the foundation of the building, else the whole will crash. I did not heed the warning and have killed my country."[66]

The country Széchényi thought he killed was only a tiny province within the vast cultural unity of the west. Today the new version of Metternich's "white and red Jacobins," twin enemies of the conservative way to freedom, are poised to kill the country once known as Europe.

* * *

In a centrifugal epoch, only an outlook of inner balance can resist this pull toward extremes and restore the magnetism of the center. A total crisis, moral, cultural, and political, requires not only action but universal principles for action. The dynamism and "vive la force!" of unprincipled men-of-action is no solution to the crisis but one of its causes. Does not history itself suggest the principles we need to analyze what is wrong and to act for what is right? By their decorum of law and form, by their insistence on ethical means toward whatever ends, reconciling tradition with reason and building on the dignity of the individual soul, the principles of an international humanist conservatism are as basic to creative statesmanship as to art. Their good sense and good taste, equally valid in poetry and politics, have been condensed into four classic lines by the great American conservative, Herman Melville:

> Not magnitude, not lavishness,
> But Form—the site;
> Not innovating wilfulness,
> But reverence for the Archetype.[67]

BOOK II

THE NEW CONSERVATISM—
WHAT WENT WRONG?

TO THE NEW CONSERVATIVE, NOT THE LEAST OF THE ILLS OF OUR SOCIETY IS A TENDENCY, AS WE WHOLESOMELY CONSOLIDATE AGAINST COMMUNISM AND OUTMODED MARXISM, TO BECOME SMUGLY UNCRITICAL AND SELF-SATISFIED, CONTENT WITH ORTHODOXY, CONFORMITY, AND NATIONAL POWER. THEREBY WE MAY LOSE OR SUPPRESS THAT FUNDAMENTAL ETHICAL AND PHILOSOPHICAL RADICALISM SO VITAL TO THE PURIFICATION OF OUR TRADITIONS.

> —PROFESSOR THOMAS I. COOK of Johns Hopkins University, leading scholar and political philosopher of the new conservatism.

. . . A TORY PHILOSOPHER CANNOT BE WHOLLY A TORY, BUT MUST OFTEN BE A BETTER LIBERAL THAN LIBERALS THEMSELVES: WHILE HE IS THE NATURAL MEANS OF RESCUING FROM OBLIVION TRUTHS WHICH TORIES HAVE FORGOTTEN, AND WHICH THE PREVAILING SCHOOLS OF LIBERALISM NEVER KNEW. AND EVEN IF WE WERE WRONG IN THIS, AND A CONSERVATIVE PHILOSOPHY WERE AN ABSURDITY, IT IS WELL CALCULATED TO DRIVE OUT A HUNDRED ABSURDITIES WORSE THAN ITSELF.

> —JOHN STUART MILL, essay on Coleridge's conservative philosophy in *London and Westminster Review,* March, 1840.

ICH BRACHTE REINES FEUER VOM ALTAR;
WAS ICH ENTZUENDET, IST NICHT REINE FLAMME.

> —GOETHE, *Ilmenau,* 1783

Chapter 1

In the 1930's, when the present author, still a student, was writing an article for the *Atlantic Monthly* urging "a Burkean new conservatism in America," and to some extent even as late as his *Conservatism Revisited* of 1949, "conservatism" was an unpopular epithet. In retrospect it becomes almost attractively amusing (like contemplating a dated period piece) to recall how violently one was denounced in those days for suggesting that Burke, Calhoun, and Irving Babbitt were not "fascist beasts" and that our relatively conservative Constitution was not really a plot-in-advance by rich bogeymen like George Washington and the Federalist party. For example, the author's *Atlantic* article, written in pre-war student days, was denounced more because the word used was so heretical ("conservative") than because of any effort by the Popular Frontist denouncers to read what was actually said. It was the first-written and worst-written appeal ever published in America for what it called a "new" conservatism ("new" meaning: non-Republican, non-commercialist, non-conformist). This new conservatism it viewed as synthesizing in some future day the ethical New Deal social reforms with the more pessimistic, anti-mass insights of America's Burkean founders. Such a synthesis, argued the article, would help make the valuable anti-fascist movement among literary intellectuals simultaneously anti-communist also, leaving behind the Popular Frontist illusions of the 1930's.

As the liberal Robert Bendiner then put it: "Out of some 140,000,000 people in the United States, at least 139,500,000 are liberals, to hear them tell it. . . . Rare is the citizen who can bring himself to say, 'Sure I'm a conservative'. . . . Any American would sooner drop dead than proclaim himself a reactionary." In July, 1950, a newspaper was listing the charges against a prisoner accused of creating a public disturbance; one witness charged: "He was using abusive and obscene language, calling people Conservatives and all that."

When conservatism was still a dirty word, it seemed gallantly non-conformist to defend it against the big, smug liberal majority among one's fellow writers and professors. In those days, therefore, the author deemed it more helpful to stress the virtues of conservative thought than its faults, and this is what he did in the 1949 edition of *Conservatism Revisited*. But, in the mood emerging from the 1950's, blunt speaking about conservatism's important defects no longer runs the danger of obscuring its still more important virtues.

The main defect of the new conservatism, threatening to make it a transient fad irrelevant to real needs, is its rootless nostalgia for roots. Conservatives with living roots were Washington and Coleridge in their particular America and England, Metternich in his special Austria, Donoso Cortés in his Spain, Calhoun in his ante-bellum south, Adenauer and Churchill in the 1950's. American conservative writings of living roots were the *Federalist* of Hamilton, Madison, Jay, 1787-88; the *Defense of the Constitutions* of John Adams, 1787-88; the *Letters of Publicola* of John Quincy Adams, 1791; Calhoun's *Disquisition* and *Discourse*, posthumously published in 1850; Irving Babbitt's *Democracy and Leadership*, 1924. In contrast, today's conservatism of yearning is based on roots either never existent or no longer existent. Such a conservatism of nostalgia can still be of high literary value. It is also valuable as an unusually detached perspective toward current social foibles. But it does real harm when it leaves literature and enters short-run politics, conjuring up mirages to conceal sordid realities or to distract from them.

In America, southern agrarianism has long been the most gifted literary manifestation of the conservatism of yearning. Its most important intellectual manifesto was the southern symposium *I'll Take My Stand*, 1930, contrasting the cultivated human values of a lost aristocratic agrarianism with northern commercialism and liberal materialism. At their best, these and more recent examples of the conservatism of yearning are needed warnings against shallow practicality. The fact that such warnings often come from the losing side of our

Civil War is in itself a merit; thereby they caution a nation of success-worshippers against the price of success. But at their worst, such books of the 1930's, and again of today, lack the living roots of genuine conservatism and have only lifeless ones. The lifeless ones are really a synthetic substitute for roots, contrived by romantic nostalgia.

Such romanticizing conservatives refuse to face up to the old and solid historical roots of most or much American liberalism. What is really rootless and abstract is not the increasingly conservatized New Deal liberalism but the romantic conservatives' own utopian dream of an aristocratic agrarian restoration. Their unhistorical appeal to history, their traditionless worship of tradition, characterize the conservatism of writers like Russell Kirk.

In contrast, a genuinely rooted, history-minded conservative conserves the roots that are *really there,* exactly as Burke did when he conserved not only the monarchist-conservative aspects of William the Third's bloodless revolution of 1688 but also its constitutional-liberal aspects. The latter aspects, formulated by the British philosopher John Locke, have been summarized in England and America ever since by the word "Lockean."

Via the Constitutional Convention of 1787, this liberal-conservative heritage of 1688 became rooted in America as a blend of Locke's very moderate liberalism and Burke's very moderate conservatism. From the rival Federalists and Jeffersonians through today, all our major rival parties have continued this blend, though with varied proportion and stress. American history is based on the resemblance between moderate liberalism and moderate conservatism; the history of continental Europe is based on the difference between extreme liberalism and extreme conservatism.

But some American new conservatives import from continental Europe a conservatism that totally rejects even our moderate native liberalism. In the name of free speech and intellectual gadflyism, they are justified in expounding the indiscriminate anti-liberalism of hothouse Bourbons and tsarist serf-floggers. But they are not justified in calling themselves American traditionalists or in claiming any except exotic roots for their position in America. Let them present their case frankly as anti-traditional, rootless revolutionaries of Europe's authoritarian right wing, attacking the deep-rooted American tradition of liberal-conservative synthesis. Conservative authority, yes; right-wing authoritarianism, no. Authority means a necessary reverence for tradition, law, legitimism; authoritarianism means statist coercion based only on force, not moral roots, and suppressing individual liberties in the continental fashion of tsardom, Junkerdom, and Maistrean ultra-royalism.

Our argument is not against importing European insights when they are applicable; that would be Know-Nothing chauvinism. The more foreign imports the better when they are capable of being assimilated: for example, the techniques of French symbolism in studying American poetry or the status-resentment theory of Nietzsche in studying the new American right. But when the European view or institution is neither applicable to the American reality nor capable of being assimilated therein, as is the case with the sweeping Maistre-style anti-liberalism and tyrannic authoritarianism of many new conservatives, then objections do become valid: not on grounds of bigoted American chauvinism but on grounds of distinguishing between what can and what cannot be transplanted viably and freedom-enhancingly.

The Burkean builds on the concrete existing historical base, not on a vacuum of abstract wishful thinking. When, as in America, that concrete base includes British liberalism of the 1680's and New Deal reforms of the 1930's, then the real American conserver assimilates into conservatism whatever he finds lasting and good in liberalism and in the New Deal. Thereby he is closer to the Tory Cardinal Newman than many of Newman's American reactionary admirers. The latter overlook Newman's realization of the need to "inherit and make the best of" liberalism in certain contexts:

If I might presume to contrast Lacordaire and myself, I should say that we had been both of us inconsistent;—he, a Catholic, in calling himself a Liberal; I, a Protestant, in being an Anti-liberal; and moreover, that the cause of this inconsistency had been in both cases one and the same. That is, we were both of us such good conservatives as to take up with what we happened to find established in our respective countries, at the time when we came into active life. Toryism was the creed of Oxford; *he* inherited, and made the best of, the French Revolution.[1]

How can thoughtful new conservatives, avoiding the political pitfalls that so many have failed to avoid, apply fruitfully to American life today what we have called non-political "cultural conservatism"—the tradition of Melville, Hawthorne, Thoreau, Henry Adams, Irving Babbitt, William Faulkner? Let them apply our classical humanist values against what Melville called "the impieties of progress." Hence the even greater relevance for the 1960's of the Melville poem with which *Conservatism Revisited* ended in 1949; thereby Melville was rejecting both bourgeois and Marxist materialists from a classic humanist viewpoint:

> Not magnitude, not lavishness,
> But Form—the site;
> Not innovating wilfulness,
> But reverence for the Archetype.

This warning was issued to both kinds of American materialists: (1) the deracinating, technology-brandishing industrialists whose so-called freedom and progress is merely the economic "individualism" of Manchester-liberal pseudo-conservatism; and (2) the leftist collectivists, imposing their unity not as a rooted organic growth of shared values* but as a mechanical artifact of apriorist blueprint-abstractions† imposed gashingly upon concrete society by a Procustean statist bureaucracy. The last-named distinction—between a unity that is grown and a unity that is made—differentiates the anti-cash-nexus and anti-rugged-individualism of "Tory socialists" (in the aristocratic Shaftesbury-Disraeli-FDR-Stevenson tradition) from the anti-capitalism of Marxist socialists or left-liberal materialists.

A scrutiny of the plain facts of the situation has forced our report on the new conservatives to be mainly negative. But a positive contribution is indeed being made by all those thinkers, novelists, and poets in the spirit of this Melville quotation

---

* Here to be defined as "archetypes."   † Here to be defined as "stereotypes."

today (whether or not they realize their own conservatism) who are making Americans aware of the tragic antithesis between archetypes and stereotypes in life and between art and technique in literature. Let us clarify this closely related pair of antitheses and then briefly apply them to that technological brilliance which is corrupting our life and literature today. Only by this unpopular and needed task, closer in spirit to the creative imagination of a Faulkner or an Emily Dickinson than to the popular bandwagons of politics, can the new conservatism still overcome its current degeneration into either (at best) Manchester-liberal economic materialism or (at worst) right-wing nationalist thought control. And only via this task can America itself humanize and canalize its technological prowess creatively, instead of being de-humanized and mechanized by it in the sense of Thoreau's "We do not ride on the railroad; it rides upon us."

Every outlook has its own characteristic issue of moral choice. For thoughtful conservatives today the meaningful moral choice is not between conforming and nonconforming but between conforming to the ephemeral, stereotyped values of the moment and conforming to the ancient, lasting archetypal values shared by all creative cultures.

Archetypes have grown out of the soil of history: slowly, painfully, organically. Stereotypes have been manufactured out of the mechanical processes of mass production: quickly, painlessly, artificially. They have been synthesized in the laboratories of the entertainment industries and in the blueprints of the social engineers. The philistine conformist and the ostentatious professional nonconformist are alike in being rooted in nothing deeper than the thin topsoil of stereotypes: the stereotypes of Babbitt Senior and Babbitt Junior respectively.

The sudden uprooting of archetypes was the most important consequence of the worldwide industrial revolution. This moral wound, this cultural shock was even more important than the economic consequences of the industrial revolution. Liberty depends on a substratum of fixed archetypes, as opposed to the arbitrary shuffling about of laws and institutions. The distinction holds true whether the shuffling about be done by the *apriori* abstract rationalism of the eighteenth century or by the even more inhuman and metallic mass-production of the nineteenth century, producing new traumas and new up-rootings every time some new mechanized stereotype replaces the preceding one. The contrast between institutions grown organically and those shuffled out of arbitrary rationalist liberalism was summed up by a British librarian on being asked for the French constitution: "Sorry, sir, but we don't keep periodicals."

Every stereotyped society swallows up the diversities of private bailiwicks, private eccentricities, private inner life, and the creativity inherent in concrete personal loyalties and in loving attachments to unique local roots and their rich historical accretions. Apropos the creative potential of local roots, let us recall not only Burke's words on the need for loyalty to one's own "little platoon" but also Synge's words, in the Ireland of 1907, on "the springtime of the local life," where the imagination of man is still "fiery and magnificent and tender." The creative imagination of the free artist and free scientist requires private elbowroom, free from the pressure of centralization and the pressure of adjustment to a mass average. This requirement holds true even when the centralization is benevolent and even when the mass average replaces subaverage diversities. Intolerable is the very concept of some busybody benevolence, whether economic, moral, or psychiatric, "curing" all diversity by making it average.

Admittedly certain kinds of diversity are perfectly dreadful; they threaten everything superior and desirable. But at some point the cure to these threats will endanger the superior and the desirable even more than do the threats themselves. The most vicious maladjustments, economic, moral, or psychiatric, will at some point become less dangerous to the free mind than the overadjustment—the stereotyping—needed to cure them.

In the novel and in the poem, the most corrupting stereotype of all is the substitution of good technique for art. What once resulted from the inspired audacity of a heartbreakingly lonely craftsman is now mass-produced in painless, safe, and uninspired capsules. This process is taking over every category of education and literature. The stream of consciousness for which James Joyce wrestled in loneliness with language, the ironic perspective toward society which Proust attained not as entertainment but as tragedy, the quick, slashing insights for which a Virginia Woolf bled out her heart, all these intimate personal achievements of the unstandardized private life are today the standard props of a hundred hack imitators, mechanically vending what is called "the *New Yorker*-type story." Don't underestimate that type of story; though an imitation job, it is imitation with all the magnificent technical skill of America's best-edited weekly. And think of the advantages: no pain any more, no risk any more, no more nonsense of inspiration. Most modern readers are not even bothered by the difference between such an efficient but bloodless machine job and the living product of individual heart's anguish.

What, then, is the test for telling the genuine from the synthetic? The test is pain. Not mere physical pain but the exultant, transcending pain of selfless sacrifice. The test is that holy pain, that brotherhood of sacrifice, that aristocracy of creative suffering of which Baudelaire wrote: *"Je sais que la douleur est l'unique noblesse."* In other words, in a free democracy the only justified aristocracy is that of the lonely creative bitterness, the artistically creative scars of the fight for the inner imagination against outer mechanization—the fight for the private life.

Chapter 2

HERE WE COME—in this distinction between art and technique, between archetype and stereotype—here we come to where conservatism parts ways with socialism, even with the attractive, idealistic, non-Marxist socialism. Up to a point they travel the same road: the allegedly "un-American" road, away from the rootless, atomistic kind of liberalism, the 19th-century liberalism (or Republican party "conservatism") that is associated with cash-nexus and with laissez-faire capitalism. Briefly, let us first note where conservatism overlaps with socialism and then where they diverge.

The greatest 19th-century conservatives—Coleridge, Disraeli, Cardinal Newman, Prince Metternich—have inveighed against this atomistic cash-nexus "free enterprise" as much as Karl Marx ever did and as much as those humane, ethical, anti-Marxist socialists (Robert Owen, Saint-Simon, Proudhon) whom Marx unjustly besmirched as "utopian." Indeed "Tory socialism" is a legitimate phrase for the great conservative social reformers, from the 7th Earl of Shaftesbury through Disraeli, as well as the necessary New Deal reforms of our own great Squire of Hyde Park. Volume X, 1960, of the new *Cambridge Modern History* (e.g., see editor Bury's comments on p. 18) considers the humane social policies of Metternich toward the national minorities supposedly "groaning under the Hapsburg yoke."

It was not just an insincere slogan when Metternich objected to capitalist dictatorship over the masses by the middle-class nationalists and liberals. His letters to his confidants, Hübner, Rechberg, and Prokesch-Osten (see the biographies of all three by F. Engel-Janosi), as well as the letters to Wrede and Guizot already cited in Book I of *Conservatism Revisited*, imply that Metternich meant what he said when calling himself a *"socialiste conservateur."* A concrete example of such conservative socialism in action is the Hapsburg relief program in Northern Italy. On such an issue, even the reactionary emperor Francis agreed with his minister. In contrast with the middleclass liberal credo of laissez faire, this Hapsburg program (which Gladstonian liberals would have denounced as "socialistic" and which Disraeli would have approved) established humane public works and social aid, resembling surprisingly—according to R. John Rath—the American New Deal. The following is from Professor Rath's monograph "The Hapsburgs and the Great Depression in Lombardy-Venetia, 1814-1818," *Journal of Modern History,* September, 1941:

> By 1817 it was estimated that the funds which the Austrian government had given for its public works program in Italy had enriched the poorer classes by Fr. 5,000,000. The Austrian policy of taking care of the destitute masses in the Italian provinces by giving food and money to those incapable of employment and providing a public works program for others, is in its general outlines surprisingly similar to the public works and emergency relief programs initiated in our own country by the Roosevelt administration. . . . The actions of Francis I, meager as they were in comparison with the billion-dollar spending of our own times, did actually save many persons from intense suffering. . . . The financial condition of the Austrian government was so precarious that actual bankruptcy was feared. In spite of numerous difficulties, however, the Hapsburg monarch did earnestly endeavor to improve the lot of his Italian subjects, the hapless victims of a great depression. . . .

Where conservatism does diverge strongly from socialism is on the issue of what will replace the "bourgeois" fragmentation of society that they both oppose. The distinction between archetype and stereotype, between "grown" and "made," makes the conservative eager to insure that the unity replacing the fragmentation be a unity that grows from traditional roots and that respects the precious pluralism of the decentralized historical landmark, the Burkean local platoon. In contrast, the forms of socialism dominant today (Robert Owen and Proudhon would have socialized differently) replace bourgeois-materialist fragmentation not with organic unity but with an equally materialistic and merely mechanical unity, coerced by a central bureaucracy and falling like a bed of Procrustes upon the individual diversity. That precious diversity gets fulfilled rather than crushed within the conservative organic unity of voluntarily shared values.

Lord Hugh Cecil's valuable little book, *Conservatism*, London 1912, best states this conservative case against socialism. Cecil states the anti-socialist case without falling into the opposite bourgeois-liberal trap (the laissez-faire atomizing trap represented by Old Guard Republicans):

> There is no antithesis between Conservatism and Socialism. . . . [But] the point which principally distinguishes their attitude . . . is a rigorous adherence to justice. It is in insisting that injustice [statist tyranny] shall not stain national help to the afflicted that Conservatism finds in respect to social reform its peculiar and distinctive task. . . . The State is a clumsy, rigid instrument, difficult to handle and operating heavily and unexpectedly. It might easily have happened that workmen would have found themselves [under Socialism] in a position unpleasantly approximating to State slavery, governed at every turn by bureaucratic regulations and, worst of all, enervated by having all the conditions of their industry ordered for them and nothing left to their own initiative and resolution.

In other words, without proper constitutional checks (meaning not only some abstract scrap of paper about liberal Rights of Man but the proper traditions to make those rights concrete) the worker will get crushed not only by the social indifference of King Log (his employer) but by the social progress of King Stork (his own government). When asked by President Teddy Roosevelt, what was the justification of Austria's supposedly outdated monarchy, the old Hapsburg emperor Francis Joseph replied: "To protect my peoples from their governments." Similarly Disraeli—like Lord Bolingbroke of the early 18th century—defended the Crown and the Established Church as bulwarks of the people's rights against ephemeral politicians. The Throne, whether Hapsburg or British, serves to moderate excesses of nationalistic or economic pressure groups against individual rights. In non-monarchic America this same indispensable protection of liberty against the mob-tyranny of transient majorities is performed by the Supreme Court, that similarly hallowed and aloof inheritor of the monarchic aura.

So conservatism fights on two fronts. It fights the atomistic disunity of unregulated capitalism. It fights the merely bureaucratic, merely mechanical unity of modern socialism. It fights both for sake of organic unity—but thereby runs the risk of creating a third threat of its own. For within its organic unity lies the totalitarian threat whenever the free individual is sacrificed totally and without guaranties (instead of partly and with constitutional guaranties) to that unity. Such a total sacrifice of individual to society took place in German romanticism; organic unity there became an anti-individual cult of the folk-state *(Volk)*. This cult took place already in the 19th century. It not only unbalanced German conservatism toward extreme statism (via Hegel) but unwittingly prepared the German people psychologically for Hitler's gangster-unity.

The proper conservative balance between individual diversity and organic social unity was best formulated by Coleridge in 1831:

> The difference between an inorganic and an organic body lies in this: in the first—a sheaf of corn—the whole is nothing more than a collection of the individual parts or phenomena. In the second—a man—the whole is everything and the parts are nothing. A State is an idea intermediate between the two, the whole being a result from, and not a mere total of, the parts,—and yet not so merging the constitutent parts in the result, but that the individual exists integrally within it.

Coleridgian conservatism, the height of the conservative philosophy, lies in the above intermediate "and yet," which saves the "individual integrally" while linking him organically. The folk-romanticism of Germany and the "Third Rome" heritage of tsarist Russia upset that balance in favor of "the whole is everything, the parts nothing," thereby paving the way for nazism and communism respectively. On the opposite extreme, America upset that Coleridgian balance in favor of "the whole is nothing" ("a sheaf of corn")—after the chaotic robber-baron individualists emerged as the real victors of the Civil War. So the proper re-balancing ("intermediate between the two") would promote an almost exaggerated individualism in Germany and Russia and an almost exaggerated New Deal unity in America, not for its own sake but to even the scales.

Therefore, in America it is often the free trade unions who unconsciously are our ablest representatives of the word they hate and misunderstand: conservatism. The organic unity they restore to the atomized "proletariat" is the providential Coleridgian "intermediate" between doctrinaire capitalism and doctrinaire socialism. In the words of Frank Tannenbaum, *A Philosophy of Labor,* 1952:

> Trade unionism is the conservative movement of our time. It is the counter-revolution. Unwittingly, it has turned its back upon most of the political and economic ideas that have nourished western Europe and the United States during the last two centuries. In practice, though not in words, it denies the heritage that stems from the French Revolution and from English liberalism. It is also a complete repudiation of Marxism. . . .

> In contrast with [communism, fascism, and laissez-faire capitalism] the trade union has involved a clustering of men about their work. This fusion [the new, medieval-style organic society] has been going on for a long time. It has been largely unplanned. . . . There is a great tradition of humanism and compassion in European and American politics, philosophy, and law, which counters, at first ineffectively, the driving forces operating for the atomization of society and the isolation of man. That tradition in England includes such names as Cobbett, Shaftesbury, Romilly, Dickens, Byron, Coleridge, Carlyle, Ruskin, Charles Kingsley. . . . The trade union is the real alternative to the authoritarian state. The trade union is our modern "society," the only true society that industrialism has fostered. As a

true society it is concerned with the whole man, and embodies the possibilities of both the freedom and the security essential to human dignity.

This Tannenbaum passage is both conservative and new. Yet it would fill with horror the Kirk-Goldwater kind of mind that today claims to speak for "the new conservatism." Such horror is not an argument against Tannenbaum nor against a new conservatism. It is an argument against the misuse of language. And it is an argument against that Old Guard wing of the Republican party which has yet to learn the anti-rightist warning spoken in 1790 by the conservative Burke: "A state without the means of some change is without the means of its conservation."

What about the argument (very sincerely believed by *National Review* and Old Guard Republicans) that denies the label "conservative" to those of us who support trade unionism and who selectively support many New Deal reforms? According to this argument, our support of such humane and revolution-preventing reforms in *politics*—by New Dealers and democratic socialists—makes us indistinguishable in *philosophy* from New Dealers and democratic socialists. Similarly our support of the liberal position on civil liberties in politics supposedly makes us indistinguishable from liberals in philosophy. Shall we then cease to call ourselves philosophical conservatives, despite our conservative view of history and human nature?

The answer is: children, don't oversimplify, don't pigeonhole; allow for pluralistic overlappings that defy abstract blueprints and labels. Trade unionists (and some of the new, humanistic, non-statist socialists that are evolving in England and West Germany) may be what Frank Tannenbaum calls "the conservative counter-revolution" despite themselves (a neo-medieval organic society) and against their own conscious intentions. Meanwhile self-styled conservatives are often unconscious anarchic wreckers and uprooters (from the French O.A.S. to America's second generation of campus neo-McCarthyites). Moreover, the same social reform in politics may be supported for very different philosophical reasons. To cite an old example newly relevant today, the support of the workingman's right to vote and right to strike by both the Chartists and Disraeli merely means that some support a reform as a first step to mass revolution while others support the same reform to woo the masses away from revolution and to give them a sense of belongingness by changing them from masses to individuals.

Finally, there is the distinction between what is done and how it is done. During the Great Depression, this distinction differentiated the conservative from the democratic socialist and from the New Deal bureaucrat even when most of us together voted the same Rooseveltian rather than laissez-faire ticket. This distinction, this need to clarify the proper use of "conservative," is found in a much-discussed essay by August Heckscher, September 1953 (in the Harvard magazine *Confluence*):

> The failure to understand the true nature of conservatism has made political campaigns in the United States signally barren of intellectual content. In debate it is difficult at best to admit that you would do the same thing as the opposition, but in a different way. Yet the spirit in which things are done really does make a difference, and can distinguish a sound policy from an unsound one. Social reforms can be undertaken with the effect of draining away local energies, reducing the citizenry to an undifferentiated mass, and binding it to the shackles of the all-powerful state. Or they can be undertaken with the effect of strengthening the free citizen's stake in society. The ends are different. The means will be also, if men have the wit to distinguish between legislation which encourages voluntary participation and legislation which involves reckless spending and enlargement of the federal bureaucracy.

It is easy to say that such distinctions are not important. A conservative intellectual like Peter Viereck is constantly challenged, for example, because in a book like *Shame and Glory of the Intellectuals* he supports a political program not dissimilar in its outlines from that which was achieved during twenty years of social renovation under the Democrats. But the way reforms are undertaken is actually crucial. Concern for the individual, reluctance to have the central government perform what can be done as well by the state or to have the public perform what can be done as well by private enterprise—these priorities involve values. And such values (upheld by writers like Mr. Viereck) are at the heart of modern conservatism. . . . So conservatism at best remains deeper and more pervasive than any party; and a party that does claim it exclusively is likely to deform and exploit it for its own purposes.

Chapter 3

NATIONALIST DEMAGOGY, whether Joe McCarthy style or John Birch style, would never have become such a nuisance if liberal intellectuals and New Dealers had earlier made themselves the controlling spearhead of American anti-communism with the same fervor they had showed when spearheading anti-fascism. Only because they defaulted that duty of equal leadership against both kinds of tyranny, only because of the vacuum of leadership created by that default, were the bullies and charlatans enabled partly to fill the vacuum and partly to exploit the cause of anti-communism. Such had been the thesis of the author's *Shame and Glory of the Intellectuals*: a thesis entirely valid for the post-war Yalta era of illusions about communism among the Henry Wallace kind of liberal and New Dealer.

Today that era is long over. It is ironic that Johnny-come-lately anti-communists like McCarthy and the Birchers did not attack New Dealers until after the latter had got over the pro-communist illusions that some of them undoubtedly and disastrously had. Today it is no longer in the interest of our two political camps to go on forever with such recriminations of the past. What is to the cooperative interest of both parties is to make sure that both are not replaced (after an intervening Kennedy era) by the "rejoicing third": some new movement of nationalist demagogy. Conservatives have no more excuse to refuse to cooperate with liberals and New Dealers against right-wing nationalist threats to our shared liberties than to refuse to cooperate against comparable left-wing threats.

Fortunately many Burkeans or new conservatives—Raymond English, Chad Walsh, Thomas Cook, Clinton Rossiter, J. A. Lukacs, August Heckscher, Will Herberg, Reinhold Niebuhr, and other distinguished names—have always been active and effective foes of the thought-control nationalists. Every one of these names achieved a record of all-out, explicit anti-McCarthyism in the days when that demagogue still seemed a danger and when it still took courage, not opportunism, to attack him. The same cannot be said of other, often better-known "new conservatives." They failed the acid test of the McCarthy temptation of the 1950's in the same way that the fellow-traveler kind of liberal failed the acid test of the communist temptation of the 1930's. Both temptations were not only ethical tests of integrity but also psychological tests of balance and aesthetic tests of good taste.

Apropos such tests, Clinton Rossiter concludes in his book *Conservatism in America*: "Unfortunately for the cause of conservatism, Kirk has now begun to sound like a man born one hundred and fifty years too late and in the wrong country." But it is pleasanter to see the positive, not only the negative, in a fellow writer one esteems. Let us partly overlook Kirk's silence about the McCarthy thought-control menace in Chicago. Let us partly overlook his lack of silence in supporting as so-called "conservatives" the Goldwater Manchester liberals of Old Guard Republicanism (as if historic Anglo-American conservatism, with its Disraeli-Churchill-Hughes-Roosevelt tradition of humane social reform, could ever be equated with the robber-baron kind of laissez-faire capitalism). Fortunately Kirk's positive contribution sometimes almost balances such embarrassing ventures into practical national politics. His positive contribution consists of his sensitive, perceptive rediscovery of literary and philosophical figures like Irving Babbitt for a true humanistic conservatism today.

Even at its best, even when avoiding the traps of right-wing radicalism, the new conservatism is partly guilty of causing the emotional deep-freeze that today makes young people ashamed of generous social impulses. New conservatives point out correctly that in the 1930's many intellectuals wasted generous emotions on unworthy causes, on communist totalitarianism masked as liberalism. True enough—indeed, a point many of us, as "premature" anti-communists, were making already in those days. But it does not follow, from recognizing the wrong generosities of the past, that we should today have no generous emotions at all, not even for many obviously worthy causes all around us, such as desegregation. Not only liberals but conservatives like Burke (reread his speeches against the slave trade) and like John Adams and John Quincy Adams (among America's first fighters for Negro rights) have fought racism as contradicting our traditional Christian view of man.

The cost of being a genuine Burke-Adams conservative today is that you will be misrepresented in two opposite ways: as being really a liberal at heart, hypocritically pretending to be conservative: as being an authoritarian reactionary at heart, hypocritically pretending to be devoted to civil liberties. So far as the first misrepresentation goes: devotion to civil liberties is not a monopoly of liberals. It is found in liberals and Burkean conservatives alike, as shown in the exchange of letters in their old age between the liberal Thomas Jefferson and his good friend, the conservative John Adams. So far as the second misrepresentation goes: the test of whether a new conservative is sincere about civil liberties or merely a rightist authoritarian is the same as the test of whether any given liberal of the 1930's was sincere about civil liberties or merely a leftist authoritarian. That test (which Senator Goldwater fails) is twofold, involving one question about practice, one question about theory. In practice, does the given conservative or liberal show his devotion to civil liberties in deeds as well as words? In theory, does he show awareness of a law we may here define as the law of compensatory balance? The law of compensatory balance makes the exposure of communist fellow-travelers the particular duty of liberals, the exposure of right-wing thought-controllers the particular duty of conservatives.

Our distinction between rooted conservatives and rootless, counter-revolutionary doctrinaires is the measure of the difference between two different groups in contemporary America: the humanistic value-conservers and the materialistic "Old Guard Republicans." The latter are what a wrong and temporary journalistic usage often calls "conservative." It is more accurate to call them 19th-century Manchester liberals with roots no deeper than the relatively recent post-Civil War "gilded age." Already on May 28, 1903 Winston Churchill denied them and their British counterparts the name of conservatives when he declared in Parliament:

> The new fiscal policy [of high tariffs] means a change, not only in the historic English parties but in the conditions of our public life. The old Conservative Party with its religious convictions and constitutional principles will disappear and a new party will arise . . . like perhaps the Republican Party in the United States of America . . . rigid, materialist and secular, whose opinions will turn on tariffs and who will cause the lobbies to be crowded with the touts of protected industries.

The Churchill quotation applies well to Senator Goldwater today. This charming and personable orator is a laissez-faire Manchester liberal when humane social reforms are at stake. But, as in the Churchill quotation, he is ready to make an exception against laissez-faire when protection of privileged industry is involved. The Burkean conservative today cherishes New Deal reforms in economics and Lockean parliamentary liberalism in politics, as traditions here to stay. Indeed, it is not the least of the functions of the new conservatism to force a now middle-aged New Deal to realize that it has now become conservative and rooted and that, therefore, it had better stop parroting the anti-Constitutional, anti-traditional slogans of its youth. These slogans are now being practiced instead, and to a wider extent than even the most extreme New Deal liberal ever envisaged, by the Republican radicals of the right, with their wild-eyed schemes for impeaching Justice Warren or abolishing taxes.

The best-rooted philosophical conservatives in America derive from the anti-material-progress tradition of Melville and Irving Babbitt; they are found mainly in the literary and educational world, the creative world at its best, the non-political world. Politics will not be ready for their ideas for another generation; they should shed their illusions on that score. The normal time-lag of a generation likewise separated the literary and university origin of Coleridge's conservatism from its osmosis into the politics of Disraeli Toryism.

Sir Henry Maine (1822-1888), one of the world's leading

authorities on constitutions, called America's Constitution the most successful conservative bulwark in history against majority tyranny and mass radicalism and on behalf of traditional liberties and continuity of framework. Later scholars like Louis Hartz prefer to derive our free heritage not from the Burkean and Federalist ideas of Adams and the Constitution but from 18th-century Lockean liberalism. Both sides are partly right and need not exclude each other. For Locke's liberalism is a relatively moderate and tradition-respecting brand when compared with the continental, anti-traditional liberalism of Rousseau, not to mention the Jacobins. So we come full-circle in America's political paradox; our conservatism, in the absence of medieval feudal relics, must grudgingly admit it has little real tradition to conserve except that of liberalism —which then turns out to be a relatively conservative liberalism.

The need for new conservatives to maintain continuity *also* with well-rooted liberal traditions does not mean conservatism and liberalism are the same. Their contrast may be partly and briefly defined[1] as the tragic cyclical view of man, based on a political secularization of original sin, vs. the optimistic faith in the natural goodness of man and mass and the inevitability of linear progress. In Coleridgian terms conservatism is the concrete organic growth of institutions, as if they were trees, while rationalist liberalism is an abstract mechanical moving-around of institutions as if they were separate pieces of furniture. Conservatism serves "growingness" and revolves inarticulately and traditionally like the seasons; liberalism serves "progress" and moves forward consciously and clearly like geometry. The former is a circle, the latter an ever-advancing straight line. Both are equally needed half-truths; both are equally inherent in the human condition, liberalism on a more rational level and conservatism on a perhaps deeper level. It may be generalized that the conservative mind does not like to generalize. Conservative theory is anti-theoretical. The liberal and rationalist mind consciously articulates abstract blueprints; the conservative mind unconsciously incarnates concrete traditions. Liberal formulas define freedom; conservative traditions embody it.

Even while philosophical conservatives support liberals in

day-to-day measures of social humaneness or of constitutional liberties against rightist or leftist radicals, the above basic contrast between the two temperaments will always remain. For these contrasts are symbolized by contrasting spokesmen in our history. George Washington, John Adams, and the Federalists are not the same as apriorist egalitarians like Paine or believers in natural goodness like Jefferson. John Calhoun is not the same as Andrew Jackson. Barrett Wendell, Irving Babbitt, Paul Elmer More are not the same as the spokesmen of our liberal weeklies or of the *New York Post*. Charles Evans Hughes is not the same as La Follette or even as Woodrow Wilson. No, the need for conservative continuity with America's institutionalized liberal past does not mean identity with liberalism, least of all with optimism about human nature, or utilitarian overemphasis on material progress, or trust in the direct democracy of the masses. Instead, conservative continuity with our liberal past simply means that you cannot escape from history; history has provided America with a shared liberal-conservative base more liberal than European continental conservatives, more conservative than European continental liberals.

This shared liberal-conservative base is a rooted reality, not a rightist nostalgia for roots, and from it grows the core of the New Deal and of the Kennedy program, as opposed to the inorganic, mechanical abstractions of either a Karl Marx or an Adam Smith. So let new conservatives stop being what they accuse liberals of being—rootless doctrinaires.

Chapter 4

IN 1962 RUSSELL KIRK published an article (in that excellent magazine *America,* Feb. 17, 1962) disassociating his conservatism and that of Senator Goldwater from the John Birch Society. Or rather, on closer reading, from Robert Welch, president of the Birchers. Does such an article really refute, as it aims to do, the sort of criticism we have been making in the preceding pages? Is there a clear recognition of—a clear break with—the thought-control tyranny that has attracted so many "new conservatives"? Or is there merely an expedient disentanglement from the disreputable? Let us see.

First of all, Kirk must be given his due. There is no doubt that, by this article, Kirk and Goldwater have broken with Welch himself. And there is no doubt that this is wise and good of Kirk and Goldwater, no matter how long overdue. To be sure, their break does not involve the kind of invective reserved by them for liberals or moderate conservatives or for any fellow Republican who deviates from their Old Guard wing. On the contrary, James Reston (*N. Y. Times,* Feb. 7, 1962) quotes Kirk as calling Welch a "likeable, honest, courageous, energetic man." And the Kirk article itself condemns Welch chiefly because his regrettable "silliness" has "become the kiss of political death" for conservatives.

This kind of condemnation sounds like something spoken more in sorrow than in anger. If the Birch Society were not kiss of death but bandwagon, would there then be not invective but either cautious silence or open praise? In other words, is not this undoubted condemnation of the Birchers utilitarian and perhaps temporary rather than moral and basic?

What forces us to ask these sceptical questions is this: the earlier silence of Kirk and most of his group about McCarthy, and their own frequent adoption of McCarthyism-minus-McCarthy. For what has been ethically corroded beyond repair is—beyond repair. If Kirk and his group had repudiated

145

McCarthy in the early 1950s—McCarthy who was dangerous, McCarthy who could strike back at them more than any Bircher, McCarthy who unlike poor Welch had a mass-base—then their McCarthy-corrupted kind of new conservatism would not be discredited today. Without trying to compete in a mutual flaunting of honorable scars, the present author nevertheless cannot help but recall the flood of abusive mail, threatening physical injury, that followed publication of his paper on McCarthy radicalism at a meeting of the American Historical Association a decade ago. The reaction was anticipated; the author's parallel attack (in *Shame and Glory of the Intellectuals*) on Communist fellow-travelers had elicited equal verbal abuse (though far less threat of physical violence). These are norms of behavior, not courage but minimum norms, for any writer not guilty of the *trahison des clercs*. The real courage was not shown by the likes of us but men like George Orwell, Norman Thomas, and Elmer Davis.

To return to what has been called the Kirk-Goldwater "courageous attack" on the Birch Society: actually the attack centers on Welch, who may soon be replaced anyhow (for having attacked too many Republicans instead of Democrats) and not on the Society itself. In fact, in the same *America* article, they take particular pains to suggest that the Society can be salvaged and need not dissolve itself *provided* Welch resigns. Kirk: "In the Birch Society, he [Goldwater] says, are many good earnest people." Cannot this platitude also be said of the Communist party? What is frightening is that these two champions of "American tradition" see nothing inherently un-American and untraditional in the concept itself (with or without Welch) of a fascist-style secret society, based on the monolithic Fuehrer principle and conspiring to terrorize independent thinking by extra-legal methods and to usurp the functions of the police and F.B.I.

Let us grant that the Birchers themselves are of scant importance (they can never become an important mass movement like McCarthyism and fascism because they are too sincerely narrow to employ the pseudo-socialist slogans—e.g., Hitler's "national socialism"—without which fascist conspiracies cannot triumph in the post-industrial world). Yet a man's attitude toward this unimportant society is indeed important. For some day that attitude may show similar indulgence or non-comprehension toward a really big authoritarian menace. May show and may already have shown. In repudiating Welch's feeble and relatively harmless form of right-wing radicalism, does Kirk go on to repudiate Goldwater for his ardent personal endorsements of the unfeeble and harmful McCarthy movement?

On the contrary, it emerges that the whole point of the Kirk article is precisely to elevate Goldwater by disentangling him from his own initial entanglement with the Birchers in the public mind. Not defense of civil liberties but defense of Goldwater is the sacred cause for which poor "kiss of death" Welch must be made to resign. One cannot but feel some pity for Welch himself, so ruthlessly sacrificed for the sake of a bigger and better Welchism.

To establish himself as the Senator's mouthpiece and court philosopher, Kirk convincingly quotes personal letters to himself from Goldwater. Kirk then concludes by unconvincingly comparing Goldwater, an enemy of social reform, with that conservative reformer, that "Tory socialist," that forerunner of Roosevelt's New Deal and relentless foe of Manchester-liberal laissez-faire economics: Disraeli. In the tone of Aristotle condescending to commend his pupil, Alexander the Great, for "growing up" and for "advancing" a grade in his homework, Kirk declares:

> American conservatives need a Disraeli. Though Barry Goldwater never will write novels, he has a political charm and acuteness not unworthy of comparison with Disraeli's. Growing up politically, he already has a better grasp of political principles than most senators ever acquire. His pamphlet *The Forgotten American* was an advance over *The Conscience of a Conservative*. . . .

Curiously enough, there really is one strong and sound pro-Goldwater argument that should be adduced (not one that his supporters adduce): namely, that he is not fanatic in temperament but easy-going, un-Calvinistic, and at times open to reality. Therefore, once in power, he might behave more sensibly, in accepting New Deal realities at home and Cold War limitations abroad, than indicated by his present rhetorical demands for laissez-faire at home and total victory abroad. This fact will some day make him the Kerensky rather than the Lenin of the far right.

If Goldwater merely represented a school of economics, he still would not be a conservative; he would be a laissez-faire Manchester liberal. But at least, like such other Manchester liberals as James Mill and the early John Stuart Mill, he would then be a protector of civil liberties. But Goldwater stands for something separate from and additional to this outdated but in no way tyrannic school of economics. He has also ardently defended the McCarthyite tyranny to the very end, backing McCarthy all over the country and voting for him when the Senate majority censured him. Kirk builds up Goldwater as a moderate by contrast with Welch: "Tolerant by nature, Barry Goldwater has spoken out with firmness against hysteria." But such tolerance, such moderation is only—by contrast. How easy to be tolerant and moderate if all you need as credential is the safe sport of baiting Welch.

Our opposition to Goldwater-Kirk and the rightist press is not primarily for the sake of "being soft on liberals." In such critiques as "Fable for Americans" on pp. 113-15, *Conservatism Revisited* is "harder" on liberals, in basic philosophical challenge, than any right-wing radical. The right-wing radical, being un-Burkean and authoritarian, opposes liberals because they are for free speech and civil liberties. The true conservative, in the tradition of John Adams and Burke, opposes liberals because they are *ineffectively* for free speech and civil liberties (ideals he shares with them). Their ineffectiveness for freedom—for example, when rationalist France collapsed in 1940 while Churchillian England fought on—comes from being rooted in the thin top-soil of 18th-century rationalism instead of the deeper and older continuity of history.

The distinction in effectiveness resembles our earlier distinction between the many written constitutions of France and the single unwritten one of England. And in America liberals were right in trying to save civil liberties from McCarthy, a radical subverter of the American Constitution. But they were ineffective in doing so (having undermined their position by themselves earlier attacking the Constitution in their anti-Supreme-Court days of the 1930's). What effectively stopped McCarthy was the conservative, Constitution-revering Committee of Senator Watkins and America's traditional old-fashioned decencies.

But are not McCarthy and his movement dead and forgotten? Is it not clear to everyone that such fake anti-communism and such Lumpen-conservatism have nothing to do with the serious anti-communism of a responsible conservatism? No, apparently not clear enough to enough people. Somehow the responsible conservatives have failed to make their disclaimer ring true in broader circles. At least the liberals, atoning for the Popular Front mistakes about communism, have by now cleaned house of fellow-travelers; most liberals by now have made their disclaimer of communism crystal-clear. In contrast, a big Chicago publisher on February 10, 1962, announced paperback reprints of "important" books espousing "the philosophy of intellectual conservatism" and headed that list with two books glorifying McCarthy. Such examples show that the ghost of McCarthy still walks and that the word "conservatism" is still linked with him in the popular mind.

For what motive do we single out Kirk among so many others? Is it to "pick" on him? Is it out of unconscious envy and malice? Or conscious competitiveness? Or is it, rather, to honor him—as the one man in his group who most merits analysis, whose early intellectual achievements are so considerable that they are only enhanced by our criticism of his later failures?

The reader will see that the last-named motive is at least partly at work if the reader compares Kirk's scholarly writings with the journalese of Kirk's fellow rightists. Kirk has been here singled out for extended analysis because he is not the least but the most respectable of "his group." And "respectable" is being used not in the stuffy sense nor in the snobbish sense but in the sense of being intellectually and ethically respectable. "His group" means that whole inconsistent spectrum of Goldwater intellectuals and right-radical magazines.

Most of them are so muddled they don't even know when they are being 19th-century liberal individualists (in economics) and when they are being 20th-century semi-fascist thought-controllers (in politics). Logically, these two qualities are contradictory. Psychologically, they unite to make America's typical pseudo-conservative rightist.

Kirk usually makes good sense about Coleridge, Santayana, and Irving Babbitt and sometimes makes good sense about Burke. For example, his sensible defense of Burke in that whole very interesting January 30th issue (1962) of *National Review*. These virtues make it all the sadder that even the best of the rightists has discredited himself. Kirk-as-thinker is bankrupt not for being wrong on some merely topical issue like his ardent and mistaken support of Nixon for President and Goldwater for Senator. Nixon was—Goldwater is—an ephemeral fad, neither so evil nor so good as their foes and friends believe; we have all been as wrong as Kirk on such shallow topical issues. Kirk is bankrupt not for this but for having been wrong—no, worse than wrong: morally evasive—on such profounder issues as McCarthyism. Finally, he and perhaps half of the new conservatives are bankrupt for succumbing to what we earlier defined as the conservatism of nostalgia, the confusion of concrete living roots with abstract yearning for roots.

How can one attribute bankruptcy to a going concern? Indeed, this new American right seems a very successful concern. On every TV station, on every mass-circulation editorial page, the word "conservatism" in the 1960's has acquired a fame, or at least notoriety, that it never possessed before. In contrast, the valid conservative philosophers who inspire the present volume—cultural conservatives like Melville and Jakob Burckhardt, liberal conservatives like the great Tocqueville, unliberal conservatives like Metternich and Gentz, and even the two Anglo-American fountainheads, Burke and John Adams themselves—never achieved a comparable circulation and audience in their lifetime. Far more millions watch Senator Goldwater being personable on television. Is this not triumph rather than bankruptcy?

But failure must be defined in terms of one's own ideal, not in terms of piled-up clippings from the mass media or attractive packaging in the picture magazines. The latter triumph is not the sort that Russell Kirk or other early new conservatives had dreamed of, by their own high ethical and intellectual standards. Although Senator Goldwater refers to Kirk as his pet ideologist, Senator Goldwater is not what Kirk was dreaming of as his philosopher-king when he first published his brilliant *Conservative Mind.* "Bliss was it in that dawn to be alive"—unblissful refrain for each generation of pawned dreams.

Which is it, triumph or bankruptcy, when the empty shell of a name gets acclaim while serving as a chrysalis for its opposite? The historic content of conservatism stands, above all, for two things: organic unity and rooted liberty. Today the shell of the "conservative" label has become a chrysalis for the opposite of these two things: at best for atomistic Manchester liberalism, opposite of organic unity; at worst for thought-controlling nationalism, uprooting the traditional liberties (including the 5th Amendment) planted by America's founders.

Chapter 5

IT IS NOT a question of equating the American right-wing threat with the stronger and cleverer threat of Russian and Chinese Communist expansion. There is a periodic liberal hysteria about "hysteria"—a witch-hunt against "witch-hunts" —that would equate the minor domestic threat with the major foreign one. But only the foreign one has behind it the powerful Red war-machine. In some ways McCarthy was not so much a major threat to liberals as he was a major integrity-test for conservatives. The pro-communist fellow-traveler kind of liberal (then influential, now not) used to exaggerate the McCarthy threat deliberately: in order to minimize the foreign Soviet threat. Analogously the American rightist has always been exaggerating the threat of the feeble American Communist party: in order to minimize the threat of Mc-Carthy-style rightists and also in order to spend less taxes and less foreign aid toward stopping the foreign Soviet threat. Thanks to the vigilance of ADA-style liberals in cleaning their own house (which is more than many conservatives have done) there is no longer any noteworthy internal communist threat. (Except for espionage—and this is best dealt with by the F.B.I., not by soap-boxing amateurs.)

A sober comparative assessment of these three different menaces would call the foreign Soviet one the greatest, the domestic rightist one the second greatest, and the domestic Communist party the least by far. But only a monomaniac concentrates on a single menace, whether the greatest or the least of these three. An effective defense of freedom—by liberals, conservatives, and democratic socialists alike—would fight on all three fronts simultaneously, though not with equal resources and never equating all three. Such a pluralism of fronts also serves the purpose of preventing the secularized messianic crusades that are the curse of the 20th century.

Even when they crusade for a good and sane end, the cru-

153

saders make it bad by their means and make it mad by their obsessiveness. It is not true that you can only defend freedom against the crusading fascists or communists by some monolithic counter-crusade and counter-ideology. Freedom's strength is precisely that it is not confined to Procrustean ideologies, that it has the classic virtues of balance, proportion, and sense of humor. (Apropos humor as an essential balancer of our Greek-derived western civilization, André Malraux finds "the secret of man in the Grecian smile" and concludes of Greek sculpture and of the entire humanist culture it symbolizes: "Much more than in its gowns, Greece inheres in the light flicker of its lips.") Totalitarianism is forced to retreat and recede, as in the de-Stalinizing renewal of the Soviet poets of the thaw and of the Poles at Poznan, not by counter-fanatics (who only egg it on) but by the pluralist and protean quality of life itself. In the end Proteus conquers Procrustes.

More important than the secular religions and political ideologies of the theorizers are a movement's actual ethical practice and cultural roots. The gifted historian Nicholas Vakar writes (in *The Taproot of Soviet Society*, 1961):

After each war they [freedom's barbarian enemies] make their grab in the name of whatever rationalization is currently popular. . . . In fact it has mattered little under what forms civilization has from time to time been defeated. The delusion that it does matter—that political *creeds* are reliable guides to the quality of political movements—is perhaps the most dangerous of civilized notions. . . . If McCarthyism had been seen culturally in its true colors, instead of in the assumed garb of anti-Communist *ideology*, it would never have climbed out of the gutter. The decent people who in honest confusion assented to chaos, saying "I don't like his methods, but—," would instead have seen at once that methods were of the cultural essence. Culturally, what the senator represented was not opposition to communism at all but another path into the same ethical jungle.

It is misleading that "conservatism" contains the suffix "ism." It is not an ism: Adams, Burke, Tocqueville detested all systems, all ideologies. It is a way of living, of balancing and harmonizing; it is not science but art. Conservatism is the art of listening to the way history grows. This sense for the rhythm of history reminds one of those miraculous peasant-poets of legend who could listen to the sound of grass growing. They "understood the language of birds"; that is, the never-articulated language of unblueprinted organic growth. This is why Metternich defined his conservatism not as any abstract system or ideology but simply as *"tout à terre, tout historique."*

Thus envisaged, not as an ism but as the history-rooted balancing and transcending of isms, there seems no doubt at all that the finest conservative episode in American history, since the miracle of the *Federalist* papers, is the 1952 presidential campaign of Adlai Stevenson. No figure in our time has better expressed the good-humored, pluralist harmonizing of isms and interests that compose the American reality. During the decade 1952-62, the creative role of Adlai Stevenson has been the perfect object-lesson of how to attain liberal and conservative synthesis: Mill plus Burke; Jefferson plus John Adams; civil liberties and open-mindedness plus a *noblesse*-obligated, traditional, and very American spirit of aristocracy, a Periclean-democratic aristocracy.[1] In careerist terms Stevenson failed; on election day, twice. But indirectly he achieved the perhaps more important success of lastingly raising the ethical and intellectual standards of both parties. That is why in the 1960 campaign Kennedy rose to the heights he was capable of, while Nixon did not sink to the depths he was capable of. Again we turn for special insight to the earlier-noted essay by August Heckscher (*Confluence*, September 1953):

Conservatism is rarely a program and certainly never a dogma. It is not an ideology. At its best conservatism is a way of thinking and acting in the midst of a social order which is too overlaid with history and too steeped in values, too complex and diverse, to lend itself to simple reforms. It is a way of thought which not only recognizes different classes, orders, and interests in the social order but actually values these differences and is not afraid to cultivate them.

. . . So persistent have been the reverberations of this [business-versus-New Deal] period that many people saw Adlai Stevenson as something close to a radical because he bore the Democratic banner. They failed to discern that he was by all odds the most consistent and philosophically mature conservative to have arisen in this century in either party. Stevenson had to a unique degree a sense of the diversity of which American society is composed. He had a feeling for the way separate groups could be brought into the service of the whole.

In 1952 Stevenson himself declared:

The strange alchemy of time has somehow converted the Democrats into the truly conservative party of this country —the party dedicated to conserving all that is best, and building solidly and safely on these foundations. The Republicans, by contrast, are behaving like the radical party— the party of the reckless and the embittered, bent on dismantling institutions which have been built solidly into our social fabric. . . . Our social-security system and our Democratic party's sponsorship of the social reforms and advances of the past two decades [are] conservatism at its best. Certainly there could be nothing more conservative than to change when change is due, to reduce tensions and wants by wise changes, rather than to stand pat stubbornly, until like King Canute we are engulfed by relentless forces that will always go too far.

And ten years later Walter Lippmann made a similar statement (equally encouraging for those of us who want to take conservatism away from the "conservatives"): "Though Mr. Kennedy is a progressive and a liberal, he is also a profound conservative, and only the befuddled theorists find that strange and hard to understand" (New York *Herald Tribune,* February 15, 1962). Despite the befuddled theorists, liberalism and conservatism in America have frequently combined in the same statesman, with Lincoln the greatest example of all and with Kennedy and Stevenson being better liberals than the Popular

Front liberal weeklies of the 1930's and better conservatives than the rightist weeklies of the 1960's.

In conclusion, let us broaden the discussion from America into certain worldwide considerations about the nature of despotism. They are considerations about which all men of good will can agree as a strategy of freedom, whether New Deal social democrats or Manchester-liberal Republicans or Burkean conservatives.

According to the neo-Stalinist wing in Russia today,[2] almost all intellectuals and reformers are secret agents of western capitalism. According to the right wing today in America, almost all intellectuals and reformers are secret agents of eastern communism. Mirror images, of course. And twice wrong.

Each mirror image needs the other and feeds on the other. They need each other as bogeymen. They feed on each other because each leftist extreme frightens waverers into the rightist camp; each rightist extreme frightens waverers into the leftist camp. McCarthyism used to frighten European liberals into being fellow-travelers with communism. Communism frightens American conservatives into being fellow-travelers with the pseudo-conservative nationalist thought-controllers.

Neither mirror image is strong enough to destroy freedom by itself. Freedom is destroyed when both attack at the same time. Lenin was able to seize power in November 1917 only because the new Duma government had been weakened by right-wing authoritarians, the John Birchers of Russia, who slandered it as "Red" and who had undermined it by the Kornilov putsch in September. Hitler was able to seize power in 1933 only because the Weimar Republic had been weakened by Communist authoritarians, who slandered it as "social fascist" and who had undermined it by post-war putsches. In 1962, in France, the anti-De Gaulle Communists and the O.A.S. rightists are examples of the same process in our own time. So are the Gizenga leftists and Tshombe rightists in the Congo. So are the alternative left and right revolts in Venezuela, 1962.

In both Congo and California, in France today as in Kerensky's Russia yesterday, the fellow-traveler left and the thought-control right are still needing each other and feeding each other, as against the center. Meanwhile in every country the Burke-style conservatives, who revere a rooted Constitution, and the Mill-style liberals, who revere civil liberties, likewise need each other: to unite against what Metternich called "the white radicals" of the right as well as the red radicals. Hence this slogan to end all slogans: LIBERTARIANS OF THE WORLD, UNITE! YOU HAVE NOTHING TO LOSE BUT ABSTRACTIONS. YOU HAVE A WORLD TO CHAIN.

Liberties versus "liberty." Concrete liberties, preserved by the chains of ethics, versus abstract liberty-in-quotes, betrayed by messianic sloganizing, betrayed into the far grimmer chains of totalitarianism. "Man was born free" (said Rousseau, with his faith in natural goodness of man) "but is everywhere in chains." "In chains, and so he ought to be," replies the thoughtful conservative, defending the good and wise and necessary chains of rooted tradition and historic continuity, upon which depend the civil liberties, the shared civil liberties of modern liberals and conservatives, and parliamentary monarchists, and democratic socialists. Without the chaos-chaining, the Id-chaining heritage of rooted values, what is to keep man from becoming Eichmann or Nechayev—what is to save freedom from "freedom"?

NOTES

Book I

Foreword

1. Oscar Wilde, *Lady Windermere's Fan*, Act III.
2. Heinrich Ritter von Srbik, *Metternich, der Staatsmann und der Mensch*, 2 vols., Munich, F. Bruckmann, 1925. I have drawn heavily on Srbik for his information, not necessarily for his interpretations and certainly not for his later politics. Biographies of Metternich in English that have used some part of the longer, untranslated Srbik documentation, include: Raoul Auernheimer, *Prince Metternich, Statesman and Lover*, New York, Alliance, 1940; Algernon Cecil, *Metternich*, London, Eyre and Spottiswoode, 1933; H. du Coudray, *Metternich*, New Haven, Yale Univ. Press, 1936; Arthur Herman, *Metternich*, N. Y., Century Co., 1932; F. de Reichenberg, *Prince Metternich in Love and War*, London, Martin Secker, 1938. Du Coudray's seems by far the best of these books in analyzing Metternich as a person. But none of these seems really satisfactory from the viewpoint of clarifying and reassessing the historical function of conservatism; and instead of using them, I have preferred to work directly from the undigested raw materials of the Srbik original and from the collections of Metternich's letters and memoirs and those of his contemporaries, such as Guizot, Hübner, Disraeli, and Heine. Automatically outdated for lack of sources are such pre-Srbik biographies of Metternich as G. B. Malleson, *Metternich*, London, 1888 and G. A. C. Sandeman, *Metternich*, London, Methuen, 1911, though Sandeman does extremely well with what sources he has. Turning from biographies of Metternich to chapter-length essays: each of the following books contains a particularly rewarding chapter on him,—Maurice Paléologue, *Romanticisme et Diplomatie; Talleyrand, Metternich, et Chateaubriand*, Paris, 1924; Albert Sorel, *Essais d'histoire et de critique*, Paris, 1883; E. L. Woodward, *Three Studies in European Conservatism; Metternich, Guizot, and the Catholic Church in the 19th Century*, London, 1929.
3. Viktor Bibl, *Kaiser Franz und seine Erbe*, Vienna, 1922; *Metternich in neuer Beleuchtung. Sein geheimer Briefwechsel mit Wrede 1831-4*, Vienna, 1928; *Metternich, der Dämon Oesterreichs*, Leipzig and Vienna, Johannes Günther, 1936.
4. His "memoirs" are not only memoirs but include his letters, the diary of his wife Melanie, his "Confession of Faith" to Tsar Alexander, his unfinished "Political Testament," etc. They were edited by his son, Prince Richard Metternich. Under different titles the same memoirs appear in English, French, and German; only the first five volumes of them in English, all eight in French and German. In my citations, the English *Memoirs* (and pagination) are used for the first five volumes, the French *Mémoires* for the last three. Prince Clemens Metternich, *Memoirs of Prince Metternich*, tr. by Mrs. Alexander Napier, 5 vols., London, 1880; N. Y., 1881 (same pagination in London and N. Y. editions). *Mémoires,*

documents et écrits divers, laissés par le Prince de Metternich, 8 vols., Paris, 1883. *Aus Metternichs Nachgelassenen Papieren,* Vienna, 1880-84. (Like many an apologia, the memoirs are often unreliable; the wary historian must assess each separate instance on its merits.)

Metternich's other published letters include: *Correspondance avec le cardinal Consalvi* (ed. Van Duern), Louvain, 1899; *Lettres à la Comtesse de Lieven, 1818-19* (ed. J. Hanoteau), Paris, 1909; *Metternich und Kübeck, ein Briefwechsel,* Vienna, 1910; etc. Some Metternich letters are also included in Count Prokesch-Osten, *Aus dem Nachlasse des Grafen Prokesch-Osten,* 2 vols., Vienna, 1881; F. v. Gentz, *Oesterreichs Theilnahme an den Befreiungskriegen,* Vienna, 1887, and *Briefe von und an F. von Gentz,* 4 vols. in 3, Berlin, 1909; etc.

5. Goethe in conversation with Soret, Feb. 3, 1830. J. P. Eckermann, *Gespräche mit Goethe,* 21st ed., ed. by Prof. H. H. Houben, Leipzig, 1925; p. 568. (Cf. the version of Soret, shorter but in this case not essentially different, in C. A. H. Burckhardt, ed., *Goethes Unterhaltungen mit Friedrich Soret,* Weimar, 1905; p. 77.)

6. Edmund Burke, "Reflections on the Revolution in France," 1790. *The Works of the Right Honourable Edmund Burke,* new edition, London, C. & J. Rivington, 1826; V, 59.

Chapter 1

1. Letter from Vienna, June 15, 1847; Metternich, *Mémoires,* VII, 402.

2. Metternich's greeting to Disraeli, quoted by Disraeli to his wife in a letter of Jan. 7, 1849. Monypenny & Buckle, *The Life of Benjamin Disraeli,* new and rev. ed., 2 vols., Macmillan, N. Y., 1929; I, 946.

3. Letter from Disraeli to Lord Stanhope, Feb. 12, 1864. Monypenny & Buckle, *op. cit.,* I, 1010. Italics mine.

4. François P. G. Guizot, *Mémoires pour servir à l'histoire de mon temps,* 8 vols., Paris, 1858-67; IV, 20 ff.

5. Gustav von Usedom, *Politische Briefe und Charakteristiken aus der deutschen Gegenwart,* 1849; p. 57. Quoted in Srbik, *op. cit.,* I, 1.

6. Quoted in Theodore Spencer's article, "Portrait: Alfred North Whitehead," in *The American Scholar,* N. Y., winter, 1946-47.

7. W. B. Yeats, *Autobiographies,* 2nd ed., N. Y., Macmillan, 1927; p. 119.

8. *The Complete Works of Thucydides,* tr. by Crawley, Modern Library ed., N. Y., 1934; p. 191, describing civil war in Corcyra, 426 B.C.

9. Metternich, *Memoirs,* III, 470; in his "secret memorandum" of Dec. 1820.

10. J. S. Mill, *On Liberty,* N. Y. & Boston, H. M. Caldwell Co., n. d.; pp. 111, 96. (The quotation in the earlier sentence is from his *Autobiography,* first published 1873.)

11. This Procrustean problem is brilliantly discussed by Francis Stuart Campbell (pseudonym for Erik v. Kuehnelt-Leddihn), *The Menace of the Herd, or Procrustes at Large,* Milwaukee & N. Y., Bruce Publishing Co., 1943. See also Mr. Kuehnelt-Leddihn's article "A Critique of Democracy," in *The New Scholasticism,* July, 1946, XX, No. 3.

12. Maine quoted and discussed in W. L. Burn, "English Conservatism," article in *The Nineteenth Century And After,* London, Jan., 1949; pp. 10-11.

13. Feodor Dostoyevsky [Dostoevsky], *The Short Novels of Dostoev-*

sky, tr. by Constance Garnett from the Russian, N. Y., Dial Press, 1945; *Notes from Underground*, pp. 142, 149. Italics mine.

14. Letter from Vienna, Oct. 10, 1847. Metternich, *Mémoires, documents, et écrits divers*, 8 vols., Paris, 1883; VII, 427.

15. *New York Herald Tribune*, book review section, Sunday, Oct. 8, 1939; p. 20.

16. Goebbels quotation from *Atlantic Monthly*, Boston, June, 1940; p. 792.

17. José Ortega y Gasset, *The Revolt of the Masses*, N. Y., W. W. Norton and Co., 1932; pp. 79-82. The Spanish original, *La Rebelión de las Masas*, was published in 1930.

18. Friedrich Nietzsche, *Beyond Good and Evil*, chap. viii, aphorism 241; p. 172 in the Modern Library Edition, N. Y. Italics mine.

19. Quotations from Jacob Burckhardt's various works, as compiled in the Burckhardt anthology *Kultur und Macht*, ed. Michael Freund, Potsdam, Alfred Protte, 1934; pp. 97-103; and in Frederic Lilge, *The Abuse of Learning*, N. Y., Macmillan, 1948; pp. 103-104. Citations from the former are translated from the German by me. Those from the latter are based on the translation of Burckhardt's *Weltgeschichtliche Betrachtungen* by J. H. Nichols, published under the title *Force and Freedom*, N. Y., 1943; pp. 24, 40, 41, 43.

20. Metternich, *Memoirs*, III, 458-60. The quotations are from his "Confession of Faith," sent as a "secret memorandum" to Alexander on Dec. 15, 1820.

21. In a letter to his Russian friend, Countess (later, Princess) Lieven. Metternich, *Lettres de Prince de Metternich à la Comtesse de Lieven, 1818-1819*, ed. Jean Hanoteau, Paris, 1909.

22. In 1819 he exulted to England's Prince Regent: "A new era is beginning, and it will be an era of salvation." "Era of salvation" recurs in a letter from Laibach, March 31, 1821. Metternich, *Memoirs*, III, 325, 527.

Chapter 2

1. Clemens Metternich, *Memoirs of Prince Metternich*, 5 vols., London, 1880; IV, 432.

2. Motto discussed in Metternich, *Lettres du Prince de Metternich à la Comtesse de Lieven*, ed. Jean Hanoteau, Paris, 1909; pp. 171-2.

3. Letter from Laibach, Jan. 10, 1821; Metternich, *Memoirs*, III, 480-81. Italics mine.

4. Count Prokesch-Osten, *Aus dem Nachlasse des Grafen Prokesch-Osten; Briefwechsel mit Herrn von Gentz und Fürsten Metternich*, 2 vols., Vienna, 1881; II, 357.

5. Part of Friedrich Gentz's famous essay, "Vom politischen Zustande von Europa vor und nach der französischen Revolution." Italics mine.

6. Alleged with fascinating evidence yet not wholly convincingly by Srbik, II, 245-86.

7. Franz Grillparzer, *Sämtliche Werke*, ed. by A. Sauer, 5th ed., III, 110.

8. Letter from Ischl, Aug. 7, 1825; Metternich, *Memoirs*, IV, 226-7.

9. A. Sorel, *Essais d'histoire et de critique*, Paris, 1883. Sorel adds: "Without a peer in his age or in his style . . . Metternich remains by

exterior grace, by the excellence of tone, the perfection of attitude, and the subtle knowledge of the proprieties an incomparable master."

10. Bibl, *Metternich,* p. 310. For Grillparzer's detailed analysis, see his essay "Fürst Metternich" in his *Sämtliche Werke,* ed. by A. Sauer, 5th ed., XIV, 151 ff.

11. For his quoting hundreds of lines of Byron from memory, see Srbik, I, 281-2. For romanticism as "anti-literature," see Srbik, I, 283.

12. Bibl, *Metternich,* p. 199.

13. C. K. Webster, *British Diplomacy, 1813-15,* London, 1921; p. 366.

14. Metternich, *Memoirs,* III, 463.

15. Heinrich von Kleist, *Werke,* Berlin, Paul Franke Verlag, n. d.; "Die Hermannschlacht," pp. 110, 114, 138; the Nazi editorial comments are from Dr. Willi Koch, p. xi.

16. Martin Greenberg, "Heinrich Heine: Flight and Return," *Commentary* magazine, N. Y., March, 1949; p. 229, col. 2.

17. Heinrich Heine, *Werke,* ed. by O. Watzel, Leipzig, Insel-Verlag; IV, 479.

18. Heine, *op. cit.,* VI, 84 ff.

19. This and all the subsequent Heine quotations are from Heinrich Heine, *Works,* tr. by C. G. Leland, V, 207-8.

20. Heinrich Steffens, *Was Ich Erlebte,* 8 vols., Breslau, 1843; VIII, 314.

21. Paul Wentzke, *Geschichte der deutschen Bursch..nschaft,* Heidelberg, 1919; pp. 118 ff., 131, 167-8, 181-3, 299-301. Heinrich von Treitschke, *History of Germany,* 6 vols., N. Y., 1915-19; II, 432.

22. This question of pre-Hitler Nazism is discussed in Peter Viereck, *Metapolitics: From the Romantics to Hitler,* N. Y., Knopf, 1941; chapter iv, "Father Jahn, The First Storm Trooper," is a far more detailed and amplified version of the present brief Jahn section. This book of 1941, which had been accepted in 1942 as the author's Ph.D. thesis at Harvard, is now permanently out-of-print. A new, revised edition, with the same pagination for references here and in footnote 27, etc., and with a new introductory chapter on the Bonn Republic, was published as a Capricorn paperback by G. P. Putnam's Sons, N. Y., 1961. The title of this 1961 edition, which is still in print, was changed to *Metapolitics: The Roots of the Nazi Mind.*

23. H. von Srbik, *Metternich, der Staatsmann und der Mensch,* 2 vols., Munich, 1925; I, 590-91, quoting the nationalist Follen.

24. Treitschke, *op. cit.,* III, 7. Carl Euler, *Friedrich Ludwig Jahn,* Berlin, 1881; pp. 180, 185-6, 199.

25. J. Friedrich, *Jahn als Erzieher,* Munich, 1895; p. 48.

26. F. Schnabel, *Deutsche Geschichte im 19ten Jahrhundert,* 4 vols., Freiburg, 1929-37; I, 306.

27. Peter Viereck, *Metapolitics;* chap. v, "Siegfried: The Metapolitics of Richard Wagner," pp. 90-125; chap. vi, "Hitler and Wagner," pp. 126-43. See footnote 22, above.

28. Alfred Bäumler, *Politik und Erziehung,* Berlin, 1937. K. M. Bungardt, *Friedrich Ludwig Jahn,* Würzburg, 1938; p. 2. Bungardt cites the Bäumler quotation with approval, also p. 2.

29. F. L. Jahn, *Friedrich Ludwig Jahns Werke,* ed. by Carl Euler, 2 vol., Hof, 1884-7; I, 164-8.

30. *Ibid.,* I, 419.

31. F. G. Schultheiss, *Friedrich Ludwig Jahn*, Berlin, 1894; p. 92. Euler, *op. cit.*, p. 376. Treitschke, *op. cit.*, III, 5.

32. Euler, *op. cit.*, p. 78. Treitschke, *op. cit.*, III, 5.

33. For Jahn's behavior in Paris, referred to in preceding paragraph, and Jahn's anti-Metternichian role at the Vienna Congress, cf. Euler, *op. cit.*, pp. 433-4, 439, 422-3, and Jahn, *op. cit.*, I, 491-7.

34. Euler, *op. cit.*, 440-41.

35. Adolf Hitler *Mein Kampf*, Reynal & Hitchcock edition, N. Y., 1940; quoted from editorial footnote, p. 19.

36. Euler, *op. cit.*, p. 445. Treitschke, *op. cit.*, III, 9.

37. Euler, *op. cit.*, pp. 483-4.

38. Jahn, *op. cit.*, I, 244-5.

39. Jahn, *op. cit.*, Euler's introduction, I, xlvi-xlvii.

40. B. Theune, *Volk und Nation bei Jahn, Rotteck, Welcker, und Dahlmann*, Berlin, 1937; p. 124. Jahn, *op. cit.*, I, 164-8. *Ibid.*, I, 160.

41. Jahn, *op. cit.*, I, pp. 417-18.

42. Paul Wentzke, *op. cit.*, p. 16. Schultheiss, *op. cit.*, pp. 83-4, 87-8.

43. Schultheiss, *op. cit.*, pp. 42, 94, 101. Friedrich, *op. cit.*, p. 25. Euler, *op. cit.*, pp. 494-510, 555-6, 562-7.

44. Euler, *op. cit.*, pp. 568-9.

45. Euler, *op. cit.*, pp. 474-8.

46. Heinrich Pohle, *Friedrich Ludwig Jahns Leben*, Berlin, 1855, pp. 321-425, contains the report made by the romanticist author, Judge E. T. A. Hoffman, defending Jahn against these charges.

47. Alfred Rosenberg, *Der Mythus des 20. Jahrhunderts*, Munich, Hoheneichen-Verlag, 1938 edition; Book III, "The Coming Reich," p. 451. As heading for Book II, Rosenberg cited the other important Nazi precursor, Richard Wagner.

48. Srbik, *op. cit.*, I, 167. F. G. Schultheiss, *op. cit.*, pp. 113-14.

49. Metternich, *Memoirs*, III, 463.

50. In April, 1849 John Stuart Mill published an essay in the *Westminster Review*, defending the enlightened parts of the revolutions of '48 but calling nationalism the "new barbarism" because it made men indifferent to the oppression of other nationalities. He foresaw nationalism as the great menace of the future. Entitled "Vindications of the French Revolution of February 1848," this essay is reprinted in J. S. Mill, *Dissertations and Discussions, Political, Philosophical and Historical*, London, John W. Parker and Son, 1859; Vol. II, pp. 382 ff.

51. Jordan's famous speech as summarized in Veit Valentin, *Geschichte der deutschen Revolution 1848-1849*, Berlin, published by Ullstein; vol. II, published 1931, p. 126.

52. Veit Valentin, *Die erste deutsche Nationalversammlung*, Munich & Berlin, 1919; pp. 46-50 deal with Jordan and are citations from the best primary source available on his speeches: the stenographic reports of the speeches and meetings at Frankfort, 1848-49,—"Stenographische Berichte über die Verhangdlungen der deutschen konstituierenden Nationalversammlung, durch die Redaktionskommission und in deren Auftrag von Professor Franz Wigard," 9 vols., Frankfurt a. M., published by Johann David Sauerländer, 1848-49, with a complete index published by the same firm in 1850. For Jordan's sacrifice of liberalism to nationalism, note I, 328, 426; II, 1143, 1146, 1150; VI, 4574, 4575; etc.

53. "Stenographische Berichte," I, 328, 426. Valentin, *Die erste deutsche Nationalversammlung*, p. 48.

54. "Stenographische Berichte," II, 1146. Valentin, *op. cit.*, p. 48. Jordan opposes "gesunder Volksegoismus" to "träumerische Selbstvergessenheit."

55. "Stenographische Berichte," I, 426. Valentin, *op. cit.*, p. 49.

56. Speech of Jan. 11. "Stenographische Berichte," II, 1143. Valentin, *op. cit.*, p. 49.

57. "Stenographische Berichte," VI, 4574-5. Valentin, *op. cit.*, p. 50.

58. A. J. P. Taylor, *The Course of German History*, N. Y., Coward McCann, 1946; p. 80.

59. Calling it a "useless scheme," Metternich describes its origins in *Memoirs*, I, 259-62.

60. "L'Italie est une expression géographique:" letter from Vienna, Aug. 6, 1847 in Metternich, *Mémoires, documents, et écrits divers*, 8 vols., Paris, 1883; VII, 415. Prokesch-Osten, *op. cit.*, II, 343.

61. "Europe has come" etc. is Metternich's comment to Wellington, 1824; Srbik, I, 320. "Atavistic attacks" etc. is Nietzsche's comment on nationalism in *Beyond Good and Evil*, Modern Library edition, N. Y., Boni and Liveright, n. d.; p. 172.

62. Tsar Alexander, whom Metternich scolded as his most backward pupil, replied docilely a few years after the Congress of Vienna: "You are not altered. I am. You have nothing to regret, but I have." Also: "You have correctly judged the state of affairs. Tell me what you wish me to do, and I will do it." For this and similar material about his treatment of Alexander as pupil, see Metternich, *Memoirs*, III, 391, 399, 495, 505-6, for the period of Aug., 1820-Sept. 1821; and Carlton Hayes, *The Historical Evolution Of Modern Nationalism*, N. Y., Macmillan, 1931; p. 118.

Chapter 3

1. Crane Brinton, "Burke the Democrat," review in *The N. Y. Times Book Review*, Sunday, March 6, 1949; p. 16.

2. For a fascinating study of Gentz, see Golo Mann, *Secretary of Europe, The Life of Friedrich Gentz*, New Haven, Yale Univ. Press, 1946.

3. Bibl, for instance, finds it "an odd irony of fate." Viktor Bibl, *Metternich, der Dämon Oesterreichs*, Leipzig & Vienna, 1936; p. 376.

4. Srbik, II, 307.

5. Letter from London, Sept. 7, 1848; *Mémoires*, VIII, 187.

6. *Mémoires*, VIII, 155.

7. *Mémoires*, VII, 640.

8. Srbik, I, 164.

9. All quotations in this paragraph in letter from Vienna, April 10, 1820; in Metternich, *Memoirs*, III, 366-7.

10. Letter from Vienna, Sept. 15, 1821; in his *Memoirs*, III, 506.

11. The above English translation of this citation (see Srbik for the detailed original German sources concerning Metternich's new constitution) is the one used in William Langer, *An Encyclopedia of World History*, Boston, Houghton Mifflin, 1940; p. 678.

12. Le comte de Hübner (A. J. Hübner), *Une année de ma vie, 1848-1849*, Paris, 1891; pp. 15-21 (March 1, 1848) and *passim*.

13. Bibl, *op. cit.*, p. 378.

14. Bibl, *op. cit.*, p. 382: "An Felix Schwarzenberg fand er vor allem dessen antipreussische Politik auszusetzen. Dem jungen Bismarck, der den alten Kanzler im August 1851 auf Schloss Johannisberg aufsuchte, erklärte er, Preussen sei noch kein saturierter Staat, es liege daher in Oesterreichs Interesse, Preussen zu saturieren; dann werde es aufrichtig und ohne Rivalität mit dem Donaureiche gehen." cf. Srbik II, 414.

15. Bibl, *op. cit.*, p. 383. Diary of the Police Minister, Baron Kempen: *Das Tagebuch des Polizeiministers Kempen von 1848 bis 1859,* edited by J. K. Mayr, 1931; p. 429.

16. Langer, *op. cit.*, p. 678.

17. Letter from Pressburg, Sept. 28, 1825; Metternich, *Memoirs,* IV, 200.

18. Srbik, II, 307.

19. Metternich, *Memoirs,* III, 386. Letter of July 19, 1820.

20. Metternich, *Memoirs,* III, 102-7; quotations about Italy from Metternich's letter of Nov. 3, 1817 and his accompanying "memorandum." Italics mine.

21. Metternich, *Memoirs,* III, 74-87; Hübner, *op. cit.*, pp. 15-18. See also Metternich's much later remarks (in 1846) on the nationality problem in *Mémoires,* VII, 212: "Réflections aphoristiques sur la situation en Galicie." A suggestive eyewitness report on why Metternich failed as a reformer is the letter of Gordon, British Minister at Vienna, to Castlereagh in 1819 (*Encyclopedia Britannica,* 13th ed., XVIII, 305):
"How much is it to be desired that the superior talents of Prince Metternich were more occupied with the revision and improvement of the administration of affairs in his own country. He is too enlightened not to perceive its palpable defects. . . . He might have courage to sacrifice himself for the institution of effective remedies, but he fears that the confiding benignity of his Sovereign might afterwards be dissuaded from the just and vigorous application of them."

22. Hübner, *op. cit.*, pp. 15-17. "Let's sleep on it" ("Darüber muss man schlafen") is cited from Anton Springer, *Geschichte Oesterreichs seit dem Wiener Frieden, 1809,* 2 vols., Leipzig, 1863-65; I, 437.

23. Metternich's sponsorship of science, art, education: Srbik, I, 298, 499, 514, 527; II, 226-31, etc. His sponsorship of commerce (railroads, merchant marine, wider tariff unions): Srbik, II, 103-5; J. H. Randall, *The Making Of The Modern Mind,* Boston & N. Y., Houghton Mifflin, 1926, p. 425; Metternich, *Memoirs,* III, 104, 106; IV, 227; *Mémoires,* VI, 305-7 & ed. note; E. L. Woodward, *Three Studies In European Conservatism,* N. Y., 1930; p. 35.

24. Srbik, I, 492-4.

25. Srbik, II, 226-31.

26. Letter from Metternich to Wrede, 1831, quoted in Woodward, *op. cit.*, p. 53. See Viktor Bibl, *Metternich in neuer Beleuchtung; sein geheimer Briefwechsel mit Wrede, 1831-4,* Vienna, 1928.

27. Quoted in Srbik, *op. cit.*, II, 298.

28. Viktor Bibl, *Metternich, der Dämon Oesterreichs,* Leipzig and Vienna, Johannes Günther, 1936; p. 380.

29. Metternich's letter to Guizot from Vienna, June 15, 1847; Metternich, *Mémoires,* VII, 402.

30. Metternich, *Mémoires*, VIII, 175.

30a. Frederick de Reichenberg, *Prince Metternich in Love and War*, London, Martin Secker, 1938; p. 434.

31. Metternich, *Memoirs*, III, 394-5.

32. Srbik, II, 511-12. According to an unverifiable rumor of the time, the Austrian diplomat Alexander von Hübner, one of Europe's last diplomats of the Metternichian school, was Prince Metternich's illegitimate son. This might add a subtle irony to the words, "I have been a rock of order," addressed to Hübner by the dying upholder of legitimism.

33. The belief that Europe needs "repose" is a leitmotif in his writings. e.g. *Memoirs*, IV, 227; III, 60; etc.

34. Cf. Guizot's acute observation: "He had no joy in fight and shunned the dangers more than he longed for the victory he might attain." François P. G. Guizot, *Mémoires pour servir à l'historie de mon temps*, 8 vols., Paris, 1858-67; IV, 20 ff.

35. Exemplified by such remarks as: "I feel the world resting on my shoulders" (Metternich, *Memoirs*, III, 390; letter from Weinzierl, Aug. 8, 1820). An entire book has even been devoted just to analyzing his conceit: Karl Groos, *Fürst Metternich, eine Studie zur Psychologie der Eitelkeit*, Stuttgart & Berlin, 1922.

36. Letter from Königswart, Sept. 25, 1819; Metternich, *Memoirs*, III, 336.

37. Hübner, *op. cit.*, pp. 15-21.

38. Seemingly the most nearly definitive study of Soviet slave labor so far is David J. Dallin & Boris I. Nicolaevsky, *Forced Labor in Soviet Russia*, New Haven, Yale University Press, 1947. The most moving and persuasive eyewitness account (the author a Jewish Polish socialist, imprisoned in consequence of the Hitler-Stalin attack on Poland) is Jerzy Gliksman, *Tell the West*, N. Y., Gresham Press, 1948. See also the following books (including some by authors sympathetic to the Soviet), listed chronologically: International Committee For Political Prisoners, *Letters from Russian Prisons*, N. Y., A. & C. Boni, 1925. V. Brunovsky, *The Methods of the GPU*, N. Y., Harper & Brothers, 1931 (labor camp memoirs of 1923). Roger Baldwin, *Liberty under the Soviets*, N. Y., Vanguard Press, 1928. Bernard Pares, ed., *Out of the Deep—Letters from Soviet Labor Camps*, London, Geoffrey Bles, 1933. Vladimir V. Tchernavin, *I Speak for the Silent*, Boston, Hale, Cushman, & Flint, 1935. Tatiana Tchernavin (his wife), *Escape from the Soviets*, N. Y., E. P. Dutton & Co., Inc., 1934. Maurice Edelman, *GPU Justice*, London, Allen & Unwin, 1938. Anon., vouched for in preface by T. S. Eliot, *The Dark Side of the Moon*, N. Y., Charles Scribner's Sons, 1947. For further sources, see "USSR: A Layman's Reading List," the bibliography compiled with a valuable commentary by Dwight Macdonald for the "USSR number" of *Politics* magazine, N. Y., spring, 1948; pp. 114-119. An essential primary source is the text of the official Russian labor code, presented last July to the United Nations Economic and Social Council by the British Labor Government.

39. Konstantin Nikolayevich Leontyev, 1831-91, quoted in Hans Kohn, "The Permanent Mission," essay in *The Review of Politics*, vol. 10, No. 3, July, 1948; pp. 283-5; italics mine. Prof. Kohn's essay, recommended for its historical insight, cites several other important

quotations (Bakunin, etc.) similar to Leontyev's. Reprinted in Hans Kohn, *The Twentieth Century. A Midway Account of the Western World*, N. Y., Macmillan, 1949; ch. vii. Equally recommended, with its different viewpoint, is Nicolas Berdyaev's brilliant study *Constantin Leontiev* (Konstantin Leontyev), available in English or French. See Leontyev's collected works, published in Russian: *Sobraniye Sochineni K. Leontyeva*, Moscow, V. M. Sablin, 1912. As for the concept of Moscow as Third Rome, a whole book would be required to do justice to its crucial psychological influence on Russian history and the Russian sense of messianic world mission. Commenting on the fall of the Second Rome (Constantinople) and on Moscow's divine mission and paving the way for the mentality of Ivan the Terrible, the 16th-century monk Philotheus wrote: "A new and third Rome has sprung up in the north, illuminating the whole universe like a sun. The third Rome will stand to the end of history, for it is the last Rome. Moscow has no successor; a fourth Rome is inconceivable."

40. From volume 29 of the collected works of Marx and Engels, published in Moscow, 1947; as cited by David J. Dallin in "Looking at the World" in *The New Leader*, N. Y., Dec. 27, 1947.

41. The film *Ivan the Terrible* was directed by the late Sergei Eisenstein. Cf. article by his friend, Waclaw Solski, "The End of Sergei Eisenstein" in *Commentary* magazine, N. Y., March, 1949; pp. 252-60. P. 259: "Eisenstein was now assigned the task of justifying Stalin's policies, particularly in the Moscow Trials . . . through the medium of a pseudo-historical film, *Ivan the Terrible*." The first part of this film, the part that was also shown in America, was shown in Moscow January, 1945, and highly praised by the official Soviet press. (The second part was to be suppressed.) Later Eisenstein fell into disgrace when Soviet authorities decided he had failed to popularize Ivan (Stalin) sufficiently, having allegedly "deliberately" created "an atmosphere of dark oppressive fear" around the reign of the glorified ruler (*Commentary*, pp. 259-60).

42. G. Fedotov, "Russia and Freedom," in *The Review of Politics*, vol. 8, No. 1, Jan., 1946; pp. 12, 33, 36.

43. For primary source on the music purge, see the resolution of the "Central Committee of the Communist Party of the Soviet Union," published in *Izvestia*, Feb. 11, 1948; English version in N. Y. *Daily Worker*, March 12, 1948. See Vladimir Nabokov's essay "The Music Purge" in *Politics*, spring, 1948; pp. 102-6.

44. Moscow dispatch of March 13 in *N. Y. Herald Tribune*, March 15, 1949; p. 17, col. 1.

45. Prof. H. S. Muller, "The Destruction of Science in the USSR," in *Saturday Review of Literature*, N. Y., Dec. 4, 1948; pp. 13-15, 63-65, describing Lysenko's use of government aid in crushing scientific independence. Prof. Muller of Indiana University is one of the world's leading geneticists, a Nobel Prize winner in physiology, and president of the 8th International Congress of Genetics held at Stockholm in 1948. During 1933-37 he was senior geneticist in Moscow. For the Communist side of the controversy, see Trofim Lysenko's own book, *The Science of Biology Today*, N. Y., International Publishers, 1949. On July 31, 1948, addressing the Soviet Academy of Agricultural Sciences, Lysenko announced that the Central Executive Committee of the Communist Party of the Soviet Union had blessed his scientific

theories, which opposed those held internationally by almost all authorities. In August, 1948, the Communist Central Executive Committee announced publicly that it accepted Lysenko's hypothesis as the official Soviet version of the science of genetics. Muller's article describes the ruthless purge of scientific dissenters. The Soviet newspaper *Pravda,* April 5, 1949, attacks Muller, in turn, as a tool of "United States imperialists." *Saturday Review of Literature,* April 16, 1949, contains debate on Lysenko between Muller and Bernard Shaw, pp. 10-12, 61, with Shaw pro. *The Situation in Biological Science,* N. Y., International Publishers, 1949, is a Soviet-approved stenographic report of the session of the Lenin Academy of Agricultural Sciences, July 31-August 7, 1948, and contains 60 addresses by Soviet scientists, including the sensational one by Lysenko.

46. Moscow dispatch of March 9 from Herald Tribune bureau, quoting M. Mitin's article of March 9, 1949, in the Moscow *Literary Gazette. N. Y. Herald Tribune,* March 11, 1949; p. 14, cols. 3 & 4.

47. Moscow dispatch of March 22 from Herald Tribune bureau, quoting Prof. Boris Kedrov's public confession, as published in letter form on March 22, 1949, in the Communist Party periodical, *Culture and Life. N. Y. Herald Tribune,* March 24, 1949; top of p. 13.

48. Hitler's attitude as summarized by his foreign minister, Ribbentrop, to G. M. Gilbert, *Nuremberg Diary,* N. Y., Farrar Straus, 1947; p. 228. Goering reinforced the same point (Gilbert, p. 85): "Stalin has been a temporizing influence in the Communist revolution. Even the Fuehrer realized that. But, as he used to say, who knows what kind of a radical may come to control if Stalin should suddenly die?" These remarks were made to Gilbert by Ribbentrop and Goering during interviews at Nuremberg, where Gilbert was prison psychologist. Separate confirmation comes from Ley, leader of the Nazi Labor Front, who wrote that Hitler's attitude toward Stalin was one of "respect, perhaps even admiration," combined with distrust of "Asiatic" Soviet Russia (Douglas Kelley, *22 Cells in Nuremberg,* N. Y., Greenberg, 1947; p. 163). Stalin reciprocated. For evidence of Stalin's long wooing of German militarism, see the Appendix on "NATIONAL BOLSHEVISM: THE SOVIET-REICHSWEHR ALLIANCE AND RUSSIA'S ANTI-SEMITIC DRIVE OF 1949."

49. Speech delivered by Andrei Zhdanov at the "Informatory Conference of representatives of a number of Communist Parties held in Poland in the latter part of September, 1947." Under the title "The International Situation," Russia's official English translation of the speech was published by the Foreign Language Publishing House in Moscow, 1947, and sold in pamphlet form by Communist bookshops in America. The quotation cited is from chapter III, p. 31 of the pamphlet. Italics mine.

50. *Newsweek* magazine, N. Y., April 4, 1949; pp. 11, 30. Page 11, top paragraph: "Soviet Anti-Semitism: . . . the director of the campaign is Alexander A. Fadeyeff [Fadeyev], secretary general of the Union of Soviet Writers," etc. Page 30, by the correspondent Edward Weintal, gives concrete evidence from official Soviet sources on the anti-Semitic meaning of the anticosmopolitan drive, most of those attacked being Jews, with the Soviet press "exposing" the original Jewish names of those who adopted Slavic names. Russia's Jews are being systematically persecuted by the Soviet press of 1949 as "homeless cosmopolitans" and "passportless wanderers," allegedly disloyal to

Stalin's revived Russian nationalism. For detailed evidence, see the Appendix on "NATIONAL BOLSHEVISM."

51. Report on the "Cultural and Scientific Conference for World Peace" in *N. Y. Herald Tribune*, Monday, March 28, 1949; p. 2, col. 5.

52. Letter from Florence, June 28, 1817; *Memoirs*, III, 58.

53. Letter to the Emperor Francis, August 29, 1817; Metternich, *Memoirs*, III, 62.

54. *Memoirs*, III, 264.

55. Letter from Paris, March 30, 1825; *Memoirs*, IV, 159.

56. From a Metternich document in the unpublished family archives at Plass. Srbik, I, 71. The tutor was John Frederick Simon of Strassburg; later editor of the revolutionary *Patriots' Weekly* in Strassburg, a follower of Marat, and finally a Jacobin colleague of some of the men of the Terror. On his tutor's leaving to join the Revolution, Metternich later made this curious comment in *Memoirs*, III, 369; April 20, 1820: "The most beautiful sun beamed on a hundred thousand enthusiasts who all believed in the dawn of the Golden Age. I was under a tutor who in the year 1793 was an intimate friend of Robespierre; . . . this tutor was the best man in the world; he wept for joy, and filled the whole world with his love and his philanthropy. I was his scholar, but, nevertheless, my heart was absorbed in misery."

57. Egon Friedell, *A Cultural History of the Modern Age*, 3 vols., N. Y., Knopf, 1931-33; III, 25.

58. Metternich, *Mémoires*, V, 410.

59. Letter to the Emperor Francis from Königswart, July 31, 1830; Metternich, *Mémoires*, V, 15.

60. Metternich, *Lettres de Prince de Metternich à la Comtesse de Lieven, 1818-1819*, ed. Jean Hanoteau, Paris, 1909; pp. 180-81.

61. Monypenny & Buckle, *The Life of Benjamin Disraeli*, new and rev. ed., N. Y., Macmillan, 1929; I, 997-1003, 1010.

62. Monypenny & Buckle, *op. cit.*, I, 997.

63. William Butler Yeats, *Collected Poems*, N. Y., Macmillan, 1940; p. 215.

64. Letter from Disraeli to Metternich, Oct. 12, 1848. Monypenny & Buckle, I, 1007.

65. Disraeli quoted by Metternich's granddaughter, Pauline Metternich-Sandor, *Geschehenes, Gesehenes, Gelebtes*, Vienna & Berlin, 1920; p. 20.

66. Széchényi quoted in Monypenny & Buckle, I, 1006; Srbik, II, 312.

67. Melville's poem "Greek Architecture."

Book II

Chapter 1

1. From appendix of the second edition (London, 1865) of Newman's *Apologia Pro Vita Sua*.

Chapter 3

1. Longer, more complete definition, with all the needed specific examples in political and intellectual life, is attempted in the first three chapters of the present writer's Anvil paperback, *Conservatism from John Adams to Churchill* (Van Nostrand Co., Princeton, N. J., 1956).

Chapter 5

1. For a full-length analysis of both liberal and conservative, democratic and aristocratic aspects of Stevenson, cf. P. Viereck, *The Unadjusted Man: A New Hero For Americans*, Beacon Press, Boston, 1956; Capricorn paperback reprint, G. P. Putnam's Sons, New York, 1962; Part IV, "The Importance of Adlai Stevenson," pp. 231-267.

2. For example, the two most recent novels of Kochetov.

Appendix of 1949 to Chapter 3,
"National Bolshevism"

Important 1962 postscript: This appendix was much
denounced by Communist sympathizers at the time. For
it was recognized as the first detailed documentation in
book-form of the officially-denied anti-semitism behind
the Stalin-Zhdanov "anti-cosmopolitan" drive of 1949,
culminating in the alleged "Jewish doctors' plot" of
1953, by which Stalin planned a big new purge just
before his sudden death. Owing to the reversal launched
by Khrushchev's speeches at the 20th and 22nd Party
Congresses, the present Communist de-Stalinization drive
admits the very same anti-Stalin charges for which the
author was denounced by Communist critics when he
made them a decade earlier. It is good to be agreed with,
even at so late a date. And, in the hope of improving
Russo-American relations and resisting a new war, it is
good to be able to emphasize that, though Russia is still
a tough undemocratic and militarized dictatorship, it has
made tremendous improvements in the thaw that followed Stalin's death. Honesty should compel us, as anti-
Communist westerners, to admit that Soviet Russia
(though unfree) can *no longer be equated with Nazi
Germany* and to admit the vast reduction in police terror, labor camps, and literary censorship in Soviet Russia.

Having been subsequently vindicated as an accurate
picture of Stalinist Russia, this appendix (*reprinted un-
altered*) is to be read only as such and not as a picture
of the changing and still unpredictable Russia of today.

National Bolshevism:
The Soviet-Reichswehr Alliance and
Russia's Anti-Semitic Drive of 1949

(This documented Appendix is in substantiation of assertions made in Chapter 3 and in footnotes 48 and 50 of Chapter 3.)

Most liberals, despising Stalinism yet emotionally committed—since Popular Front days—to the notion that it is "basically different" from Hitlerism, still cite racial tolerance as this one remaining "difference." They ignore the important post-war evidence[1] to the contrary. Racial equality is guarantied emphatically by the Soviet constitution. But so are free speech and free elections.

This switch to anti-semitism for home consumption, concealed and denied by Moscow censorship for foreign consumption, deserves detailed consideration by the conservers of freedom. For it may throw new light on what the enemies of freedom have in common. Limitless national sovereignty to wage aggressive war; anti-cosmopolitanism in culture; rejection of the humane Christian ethics with its respect for the individual; and anti-semitism: such was the German revolt against Europe, 1815-1945, whose menace the conservative Metternich was the first to foresee. Today these selfsame attitudes are part of the Bolshevik revolt against Europe, whose menace the conservative Churchill was among the first to expose, at its birth and again in 1946, just as he exposed the Hitler menace long before Munich. For these three accurate prophecies Churchill, who had introduced minimum-wage laws and a prototype of the Wagner Act a generation before the American New Deal, was thrice rewarded—1918, 1938, 1946—with the epithet "reactionary war-monger."

That anti-semitism is paired with anti-Christianity in both brands of totalitarianism is logical in view of the cosmopolitanism of Christianity and in view of its Hebrew origins. In

173

the words of the late Pope, "We are all Semites spiritually;" on this, tolerant Protestants and tolerant Catholics may agree, as well as on their joint stand against communist materialism.

During the current anti-cosmopolitan purge of 1949, the Soviet press has attacked both non-Jews and Jews but in significantly different proportions. What proportion was Jewish? Estimates vary, but in any case a large enough majority to establish anti-semitism and rule out coincidence in a country whose Jewish population is around 1%. Estimates range from Edward Weintal's 49 out of 50 to Prof. Harry Schwartz's more cautious and convincing 60%, the former statistics covering only March and Feb., the latter more inclusive: "Of more than 100 Soviet intellectuals publicly criticized in exportable newspapers and magazines for 'groveling before the west' and other 'cosmopolitan' errors, persons with apparently Jewish names constituted about 60%."[2]

That this is a coordinated drive is indicated by the fact that the victims are consistently attacked with the same two phrases: "passportless wanderers" and "homeless cosmopolitans." The Communist press makes clear the Jewish origin of many accused by revealing the original "foreign" Jewish name in parentheses after any adopted Slavic name. (This traditional device to inflame race prejudice had been used against the Bolsheviks themselves by anti-semitic White Russians in the days of Lenin and Trotsky.) Current examples follow.

The Soviet *Literary Gazette,* Feb. 12, 1949, denounces the "malignant putrid story written by homeless cosmopolitan Melnikoff (Mehlmann)." In a later issue, it "exposes" a critic with the Russian name Kholodoff as the "homeless cosmopolitan" Meyrovich. The epithet recurs when *Pravda Ukrainy,* Feb. 19, unmasks three literary critics with the Russian names Stebun, Burlachenko, and Sanoff as the "homeless cosmopolitans" Katzenellenbogen, Berdichevsky, and Schmulson.[3] Perhaps that most "homeless" of "cosmopolitans" and "passportless wanderers," Karl Marx, prophesied more truly than he knew when he said, "I am not a Marxist."

On Feb. 17, 1949 the secretary of the Byelo-Russian Communist Party said: "Only one theater in the Byelo-Russian

Republic—a Jewish one—puts on unpatriotic plays in which life in America is praised."[4] Meanwhile, ever more Jewish intellectuals are being arrested. Russia's sole Yiddish-language daily, *Einigkeit,* has been recently suspended.[5] Hebrew-language periodicals have long been prohibited, Zionism itself being illegal since almost three decades. In early 1949 the Soviet *Literary Gazette* published a key article attacking Zionism as a "bacterial weapon in the West's war against the Soviet Union and the people's democracies."[6] According to a first-hand account of Soviet slave-labor camps by the Zionist leader, Dr. Julius Margolin, "An entire generation of Zionists has died in Soviet prisons, camps and exile."[7]

When Stalin and Hitler together conquered Poland in 1939, 350,000 Polish Jews fled into Russia. Some Stalin forcibly returned to Hitler and his gas chambers.[8] Most were sent by the Soviet dictator into forced-labor camps, under the usual unbearable conditions. A majority of those who fled Hitler's brand of death probably met death in Russia; 200,000 in the estimate of the *American Jewish Year Book, 1947-1948.*[9] A Jewish refugee from the Soviet, arriving in Palestine in 1945, has described the pogroms that censorship is concealing from the west, including the public murder of 16 Jews in the Ukrainian city of Kiev.[10]

The Ukraine had been occupied by the Nazis. Presumably its present anti-semitism stems not only from the Soviet government, or from tsarist days, but from a non-Russian propaganda heritage left by the invaders. The Nazis, however, cannot be used to explain the current anti-semitic, anti-cosmopolitan drive in the uninvaded portions of Russia and in an official government-controlled press.

Anti-Zionism, which is nothing new in the Soviet government, must not be confused with anti-semitism, which is sensationally new. As an anti-nationalist, Lenin was anti-Zionist while outlawing anti-semitism. As nationalists, the present Soviet bureaucrats are anti-semitic as well as anti-Zionist. The return to Russia's deep-rooted anti-semitism of tsarist days had already begun with the Soviet slurs on the racial origins of Trotsky, Zinoviev, Kamenev and others during the famous purge of Lenin's Old Bolsheviks. By these "trials" of the 1930's, Stalin, among other things, was eliminating in advance any internationalist Marxist opposition at home to his persistent wooing of Nazi militarism. As scapegoats he was accusing his Old Bolshevik victims—again, among other things—of his own unsuccessful pro-German orientation, which at that date was being rebuffed by Hitler. Stalin's anti-Nazi "Popular Front" policy in the west during the '30s not only was a wise reinsurance against Hitler's appetite for the Ukraine. It also was a shrewd way of increasing Soviet bargaining power with Hitler by publicly blackmailing him into considering Stalin's private alliance offers during those same '30s. The greater Stalin's nuisance potential—for example, in slowing up Axis aggressions against Loyalist Spain—the greater the price he could demand from Hitler when in 1939 their alliance was finally consummated. As a result, the price successfully exacted by this Janus-faced Soviet *Realpolitik* was high indeed, Hitler being forced not only to share the spoils of Poland but to allow Soviet conquests in the Balkans, the Baltic, and Finland.

In 1941 Russia's ruler fought Hitler not as an anti-fascist but because he had no choice, being attacked. This cost millions of innocent Russian lives that might have been saved if both Chamberlain and Stalin had stopped the unappeasable Nazi earlier when Churchill warned them to. Stalin's 1939 alliance with Hitler was not an angry short-term reaction to the western crime of Munich but a calculated long-term culmination of the secret Reichswehr-Soviet military coöperation begun by the Rapallo pact of 1922 and the Berlin treaty of 1926. This coöperation is thoroughly confirmed from such entirely separate sources as the posthumous papers of General von Seeckt,[11] the 1948 memoirs of Ruth Fischer,[12] and others.[13]

In some ways a precursor of Nazi militarism, Seeckt in the 1920's organized the Reichswehr rearmament on Soviet soil, which enabled Germany to violate the disarmament provisions of Versailles behind the Iron Curtain. Already then, Seeckt planned a joint Soviet-German attack on Poland, such as eventually started off World War II. His confidential papers were captured with the German Army archives by American troops after the war and are now stored in Washington in the National Archives Building. There they are accessible to any interested historians. Some of the more sensational papers, confirming the above allegations, have been published by Melvin Lasky and Julius Epstein in *Der Monat*.[14]

Ruth Fischer is the sister of Gerhart Eisler, the Kremlin agent. She was General Secretary of the German Communist Party and a member of the Comintern presidium and knew personally the Soviet leaders, including Stalin. In his preface to her memoirs, Harvard's historian of Germany, Sidney B. Fay, vouches for the general historical validity of her assertions about Soviet-German coöperation, which are confirmed by independent sources. Insufficiently devoted to Russian nationalism, she was forced out of the Communist party by Moscow's Stalinist faction in 1926. Meanwhile, the rank and file of her fellow German Communists, not to mention western Communists, were kept in ignorance of the Reichswehr alliance. They sincerely believed that Communism was fighting against German "fascist militarism." According to her summary,

He [Communist Deputy Torgler] said: if our rank and file ever learned of these facts, there would be a mass exodus from the party. . . . In 1928, there were at least 800 men assigned by the Reichswehr Ministry to work with the Red Army. . . . In Leningrad, Perm, Sverdlovsk, and the Ukraine, munition plans were set up and run with expert German assistance. . . . The continued collaboration between the two armies has remained one of the best-kept secrets of contemporary history. In this relationship, we must seek the basic explanation of many factors of both Stalinism and Nazism. . . . After Hitler came to power, Stalin tried incessantly via army channels to get an alliance with Nazi Germany, a policy that reached its fruition finally in August, 1939. . . . Manipulated from Moscow, [the German Communist Party] was directed into a policy of silent agreement, not disturbed by name-calling, with the Nazis, and virulent opposition to the Democrats and

Social Democrats. . . . The anti-Nazis camp was split down the middle, split by an ax wielded by Stalin.[15]

The climax of this long Bismarckian tradition of coöperation between German and Russian militarism was reached in their conquest of Poland and the Baltic states in 1939 and in Molotov's eloquent speech to the Supreme Soviet:

> One swift blow to Poland, first by the German Army and then by the Red Army, and nothing was left of this ugly offspring of the Versailles Treaty. . . . Germany is . . . for peace, while Great Britain and France, which but yesterday were declaiming against aggression, are . . . opposed to the conclusion of peace. . . . There is absolutely no justification for a war . . . under an ideological flag. . . . One may accept or reject the ideology of Hitlerism as well as any other ideological system; that is a matter of political views. . . . It is, therefore, not only senseless but criminal to wage such a war as the war for "the destruction of Hitlerism," camouflaged as a fight for "democracy" . . . It is the fear of losing world supremacy that dictates to the ruling circles of Great Britain and France the policy of fomenting war against Germany. . . . Today our relations with the German State are based on our friendly relations, on our readiness to support Germany's efforts for peace. . . . We have always held that a strong Germany is an indispensable condition for a durable peace in Europe.[16]

The ripening of this Rapallo spirit was further illustrated in 1939 by Stalin's famous toast ("I know how much the German people loves its Fuehrer; I should like, therefore, to drink to his health")[17] and by Stalin's telegram to Ribbentrop hailing the cementing of their alliance by Polish blood ("The friendship of the peoples of Germany and of the Soviet Union, cemented by blood, has all grounds to be prolonged and stable").[18] Earlier, the N. Y. *Daily Worker* boasted: "If London and Paris are counting on their blockade and talk of shortage of raw materials in Germany as a means of continuing the imperialist war, the Soviet Union will soon remedy that."[19] The Soviet Union's "remedy" of sending raw materials to Germany[20] was of impressive aid to the Nazi war machine, for which Molotov claimed some of the credit after the fall of France when he insisted that "the German-Russian agreement had not been without influence upon the great German victories."[21]

The Nazi archives, captured by the American Army, contain a memo to the German Foreign Office from the Nazi expert on trade with Russia. This shows that during the first four months of 1941 Stalin sent Hitler 232,000 tons of petroleum, fuel needed by Nazi bombers and submarines to smash the lone resistance of democratic England. The same important memo praises the Communist authorities for sending the Nazis an unusually large quantity of grain and petroleum during the month of April, 1941:

> STATE SECRET. SECOND MEMORANDUM ON THE STATUS OF GERMAN-SOVIET TRADE RELATIONS. . . . The status of Soviet raw material deliveries still presents a favorable picture. Of the most important raw materials, the following deliveries were made in April [1941]: Grain 208,000 tons; Petroleum 90,000 tons; Cotton 8,300 tons. . . . Total deliveries in the current year amount to: Grain 632,000 tons; Petroleum 232,000 tons; Cotton 23,500 tons; Manganese ore 50,000 tons; Phosphates 67,000 tons; Platinum 900 kilograms. . . . The quantities of raw materials now contracted for are being delivered punctually by the Russians, despite the heavy burden this imposes on them.[22]

The irony is that some of these Russian deliveries were to be used against Russia herself, being delivered on the eve of Hitler's surprise attack and at a time when the attack had already been decided on.[23] Nor was the Soviet aid to Hitler only economic. After the two armies, which had built each other up in the 1920's, fulfilled Seeckt's original plan of conquering Poland together, "Stalin provided Hitler with a naval base near Murmansk, where the Nazi commerce raiders were outfitted. Icebreakers from the Communist fatherland cleared the way for the Nazi cruisers across the Arctic Ocean to the

Bergen Sea, making possible the very successful German raids on Pacific shipping in 1941."[24]

The argument that Stalin was merely "playing for time" for "the inevitable conflict" was advanced by Soviet apologists *after* Germany's attack. But why needlessly send so much petroleum and other military aid to someone whom you expect to use it against you? The evidence about 1922-40 makes a seriously-intended long-term collaboration (though never without mutual distrust) a more plausible explanation for the behavior of both the Soviet ruling caste and the Reichswehr military caste. Unlike the irrationally aggressive Hitler, both these castes were motivated by a non-ideological *Realpolitik* of material self-interest, as expressed by Molotov in July, 1940: "[Stalin] knew several leading German statesmen well. . . . Stalin was not of the opinion that German military successes menaced the Soviet Union and her friendly relations with Germany. These relations were *not based on transient* circumstances but on the *basic national interests* of both countries."[25] A leitmotif of the captured Nazi-Soviet documents is that Stalin "personally always advocated a friendly relationship between Germany and the Soviet Union"[26] and "was a convinced adherent of the Axis and an opponent [*Gegner*] of England and America."[27]

But at the same time Germany and Russia both displayed that increasing momentum of expansion which makes peace so difficult with any dynamic totalitarian society. This is more obviously true of the unappeasable Nazi dreams of world conquest. But Russia's urge to expansion also overreached itself in the famous Molotov-Hitler conversations[28] of November, 1940 in Berlin. Here Molotov announced Stalin's demand (unacceptable to Hitler) for control of the Dardanelles and of Bulgaria and Finland, naming this as Communist Russia's price for entering "as a partner" the Nazi-Fascist-Japanese "Tripartite Pact" against the United States and Britain. The minutes of the Berlin meeting of Nov. 12 concluded:

It was a matter [according to Hitler] of opposing any attempt on the part of America to "make money on Europe." The United States had no business either in Europe, in Africa, or in Asia. Molotov expressed his agreement with the statements of the Fuehrer regarding the role of America and England. The participation of Russia in the Tripartite Pact appeared to him entirely acceptable in principle provided that Russia was to coöperate as a partner and not merely as an object. In that case he saw no difficulties in the matter of participation of the Soviet Union in the common effort. . . .[29]

At this point the Hitler-Molotov conversation was unexpectedly broken off because of the possible danger of a sudden "air raid alarm,"[30] a dramatic reminder from the west. Next day the negotiations for Russia's axis membership were resumed. They broke down mainly because of Russian insistence on the Dardanelles and adjacent Bulgaria; this demand, as the captured records make clear, did more than any ideological difference to turn Germany against Russia.[31] Hitler became convinced there was no room for two such expansive empires. Here is how Ribbentrop summed up the failure of the November negotiations to the Japanese Foreign Minister Matsuoka in Berlin, March 28-29, 1941:

Russia would also have joined the Tripartite Pact [the Nazi-Fascist-Japanese alliance against England and America], but her conditions could not be met. . . . The third condition had as its subject the establishment of bases on the Dardanelles. . . . Germany preferred the Dardanelles to remain in the hands of the Turks. Besides, she could not permit a penetration of the Russians into the Balkans. However, Russia kept trying to push forward in that direction.[32]

Here history repeated itself. The same Dardanelles demand by the Russian Tsar Alexander—provoking Napoleon's comment that "Constantinople is the key to world empire"— helped cause Napoleon to break that earlier pact between two apparently opposite ideologies, which had caused the same surprise in its own day and which had the same aftermath in an arrogant invasion of quicksand.

By repudiating the Soviet pact, Hitler was repudiating not

only the Russians but the advice of his own Reichswehr. This culminated in Hitler's hanging of some of his top generals as pro-Russian after July, 1944. Hitler's betrayal of his relatively loyal Soviet ally was the miracle that saved the west. The west might otherwise have found a German-Russian alliance as unbeatable as the geopolitician Haushofer predicted. Today the west may still find it so, and sooner than generally realized. The Soviet lifting of the Berlin blockade in May, 1949 may be the first step toward renewing this alliance through an independent centralized German government, unoccupied by western troops. Such a government, being inevitably nationalistic, would enable the two extremes of Communists and of militarist and monopolist reactionaries to renew their Seeckt-minded pro-eastern coalition against the moderate pro-western middle group of parliamentary capitalists and parliamentary socialists.

After Hitler defied Reichswehr advice by breaking this alliance in 1941, it was revived without Hitler by the captured Reichswehr officers of Stalin's "Free Germany Committee" of 1943 and by some of the high generals in the anti-Hitler putsch of July 20, 1944. Today the alliance lives on in Germany's Russian-directed "Socialist Unity Party," openly recruited from both Communists and Nazi S.S. men. The popular appeal of this party is, as might be expected, based on "socialism" and nationalism; also, on occasion, on antisemitism, directed against leaders of the German Social Democrats. On June 23, 1948 the Berlin Communists invaded the City Assembly to intimidate it. One of the legislators the Communists beat up was the Socialist leader, Jeannette Wolff. The woman whom they struck and whom they mocked as "old Jewess," happens to be a cripple who had spent six years in a Nazi concentration camp, where her family was burnt in ovens by such S.S. men as now staff the German Communist party.

Following Stalin's liquidation of Lenin's associates Trotsky, Kamenev, and Zinoviev, no Jew remains in the Politburo—except for Stalin's protected brother-in-law, Kaganovich.[33] No Jew retains any top diplomatic post since the ousting of Litvinov and Maisky, over which the Nazis gloated so.[34] In November, 1947 the heads of the Soviet Jewish Anti-Fascist

Committee, a Committee now dissolved, were reported as complaining of the "unpublicized but nevertheless effective anti-Jewish policy which was first adopted by the Soviet government at the time of the Soviet-Nazi 1939 pact . . . and has now been revived as a corollary to the Soviet anti-western campaign. Under this policy Jews are to be eliminated from the armed services, from positions of influence on the masses, and from any activities which would bring them in touch with foreigners . . . Jews have been barred from the diplomatic and language schools and from military academies. Jews holding positions of chairman of party or government committees have now been replaced."[35]

Reports are now leaking out about the forcible mass-deportation of Jews from western Russia into Siberia. According to a scholar of the Yiddish Scientific Institute, "The Jews are being driven out of the Ukraine and White Russia by the tremendous upsurge of anti-semitism there. . . . It is, therefore, understandable that they [the Soviet government] should 'mobilize' the Jewish masses for migration to Biro-Bidjan. 'Mobilize' [the official Soviet word used] is a softer word than 'deportation,' but the sense is much the same."[36] Meanwhile *Yale Review*, usually reliable, has published an eye-witness account of the grim 1948 reality of Biro-Bidjan, Siberia's "model Jewish homeland," and of the terror of Jews in western Russia at the prospect of being shipped there.[37]

Since news must filter through so iron a curtain, skepticism must apply to anti-Soviet as well as pro-Soviet reports. However, Soviet periodicals may be found and checked in American libraries; and the separate eye-witness accounts of anti-semitic rioting by separate Jewish refugees tend to give a consistent story.[38] The new Communist version of genetics, proclaimed through Lysenko, would establish "innate master and subject races."[39] Thereby, the Lysenko case not only facilitates the Soviet suppression of objective scientific research but may conceivably provide a genetic sanction for racial discrimination. Here is the situation of 1949 as pictured by a refugee who was still in Moscow on March 15:

All the papers are full of exposés of the "rootless cosmopolites," who . . . invariably turn out to be Jews. . . .

A Jewish pogrom is in progress throughout the land, directed particularly against the Jewish intelligentsia. However, it is not a usual pogrom, from below, but a planned and directed drive from above, carried on under instructions from the Kremlin.[40]

Having earlier disposed of cosmopolitans in science, music, and literature, the cultural purge turned to architecture in April, 1949, when the Moscow journal *Soviet Art* denounced disciples of Moises Gintsburg and several other Jewish architects for cosmopolitan servility toward "soulless American architecture." The magazine itself is being reorganized for having been unnationalistic, "a tribune of slanders against Soviet architecture." In a recantation, *Soviet Art* officially announced that "hostile activities of bourgeois cosmopolitans will be unmasked to the end" and that the Soviet Academy of Architecture is likewise being reorganized to purge its "cosmopolitans," a purge believed to be "directed principally against Jews."[41] Meanwhile, "limitations had been placed upon Jewish admissions to higher schools and universities," accompanied by "steady progress during 1948 in removing Jews from leading Soviet official and economic positions."[42]

During the Munich pact days, the isolationist mind in America kept an easy conscience by doubting Hitler's concentration camps and dismissing the evidence of Nazi atrocities as propaganda and American "war hysteria." Today the same kind of mind is welcome to dismiss the evidence about Russia but only at the price of the same aftermath.

What of Stalin himself? His little-known "Report on the London Congress," published in 1907 in the *Bakinskii Proletarii*, does not increase his publicized reputation for racial tolerance:

Not less interesting is the composition of the Congress from the standpoint of nationalities. Statistics showed that the majority of the Menshevik faction consists of Jews . . . On the other hand, the overwhelming majority of the Bolsheviks consists of Russians . . . For this reason, one of the Bolsheviks observed in jest (it seems Comrade Aleksinsky) that the Mensheviks are a Jewish faction, the

Bolsheviks a Russian faction, whence it wouldn't be a bad idea for us Bolsheviks to arrange a *pogrom in the party.*[43]

On this "jest," for which Stalin saw fit to find space in a brief report, Bertram Wolfe comments: "We leave it to the reader to judge the factional purpose of this coarse-grained jest and its possible effect in a Russia that had just gone through three years of Jewish pogroms, and in a paper designed for the Caucasian storm-center of national antagonism."[44]

On the other hand, Stalin strongly opposes persecution in vastly more numerous passages, including those following the above quotation, as well as in his book on national minorities. The 1949 Stalin-prize awards did include Jewish winners, as correctly stressed in a rebuttal on this subject in the *Daily Worker.*[45] The ban on anti-semitism remains in the Soviet constitution. Kaganovich remains in the Politburo. To exaggerate the anti-semitic consequences of national bolshevism is just as unrealistic as to ignore them. The nationalism is primary; its anti-semitic corollary is merely secondary and likely to fluctuate.

Whatever the future may bring regarding Soviet anti-semitism in particular, the Soviet ruling class can be expected to continue its intolerant nationalism in general. Having the least individual freedom and lowest standard of living of any industrial country in the world, Stalin's USSR needs scapegoats to divert mass misery. Cosmopolitanism is the obvious scapegoat for any fanatic nationalism. This holds true of the recent German as well as Soviet national mission of world conquest: the two deadliest blows to civilization since the barbarian conquest of Rome brought about those other Dark Ages. Humanity's crucial choice today between nationalism and civilized cosmopolitanism is the same choice that the conservative cosmopolitan Metternich faced a century ago and justifies not a few of his warnings.

Notes to Appendix

1. For readers interested in checking the most recent material on Soviet anti-semitism, the author has prepared the following bibliography (as of June 11, 1949), still far from complete, of recent articles

on this subject. This material is still too new to have appeared in book form prior to the present book.

In early 1949 the official Soviet press began its coördinated nationalistic attack on cosmopolitans in general and (in perhaps 60% of the cases) on Jewish intellectuals in particular. *Crocodile (Krokodil)*, Moscow, Russia's leading humor magazine, featured cartoons against "cosmopolites" and "passportless wanderers," caricatured as hook-nosed, etc., on March 10, pp. 8 and 9; March 20, pp. 1 and 10, etc. The *Literary Gazette (Literaturnaya Gazeta)* of Feb. 12 exposed the Jewish last names of certain cosmopolitans and attacked the cosmopolitanism and undue attention to Jewish literature in the projected glossary of the 2nd edition of the "Large Soviet Encyclopedia;" the issue of March 9 exposed the original names of the cosmopolitan writers Zhadanov and Martich as Lifshitz and Finkelstein, etc. The *Literary Gazette* of March 2 and *Pravda* of Jan. 28 attacked the drama critic E. Gurvitch for lacking and deriding Russian national character. *Culture and Life* of Jan. 30 exposed E. Kholodov as an "anti-patriot" named "Meyerovitch." *Soviet Art* of Feb. 19 attacked Altman for "hating everything Russian" and "toadying slavishly to the west;" and in April attacked Moises Gintsburg and other Jewish architects for cosmopolitan imitation of America. *Vechernaya Moskva* of March 14 attacks the "glorification of the Jewish religion" in a book by Alexander Isbakh and mentions that his real name is Isaac Bakrakh. *Komsomolskaya Pravda* of March 6 gives the original Jewish names of Soviet sports writers whose accounts of athletic contests allegedly lack patriotic fervor. *Pravda Ukrainy* of Feb. 19 gives the original Jewish names of three "homeless cosmopolitan" literary critics. Any number of similar examples have been noted in the Soviet press.

The magazine *Bolshevik* of May, 1949, official monthly organ of the Communist Central Committee, attacked as "rootless," "unpatriotic," and "cosmopolitan" the Russian historians named I. Mintz and N. Rubinstein and the professors of economics named I. Blyumin, D. Rosenberg, and B. M. Shtein. *Bolshevik* asserts that the late economist John Normano, with whom Shtein's ideas are linked as "cosmopolitan," is really named "Levin" (*Bolshevik* gives the latter name in parentheses), an assertion originally made by the Nazi government in 1933 when Normano fled from Germany to America as a refugee; Normano denied this Nazi assertion at the time.

Bulletin of the Joint Rescue Committee of the Jewish Agency for Palestine, March, 1945; pp. 19 ff. (eye-witness account of Ukraine pogroms); April, 1945, p. 21; May, 1946, pp. 9 ff.; August, 1947, p. 13; etc.

Dovid Leibovich, "Bay Kossove in Polesy" ("Near Kossovo in the Polesye Region"), article in *Fun Letsn Khurbn: Tsaytshrift far Geshikhte fun Yidishn Lebn baym Natsi-Rezhim*, Munich, No. 6, August, 1947; p. 50 mentions anti-semitism of Soviet-organized partisans who left Jews to be massacred by German invaders. Moshe Kaganovich, *Der Yidisher Ontayl in Partizaner-Bavegung fun Sovet-Rusland* ["The Participation of Jews in the Partisan Movement of Soviet Russia"], published by the Central Historical Commission of the Partisan Federation *Pachach* in Rome, Italy, 1948.

Yale Review, New Haven, summer, 1948; Frederick C. Barghoorn, "Notes on Life and Travel in Russia" (personally visited Biro-Bidjan).

American Jewish Year Book, 1947-1948; includes G. J. Gliksman's figures on mass-deaths of Polish Jews in Soviet labor camps, etc.

Modern Review, a monthly ed. by Raphael Abramovitch & published by American Labor Conference on International Affairs, N. Y.; vol. II, No. 7-8, Jan., 1949; Solomon M. Schwarz, "The Soviet Partisans and the Jews" (cites valuable primary sources on Soviet anti-semitism), pp. 387-400.

Commentary, published by American Jewish Committee, N. Y.: Prof. Harry Schwartz, "Has Russia Solved the Jewish Problem?" Feb., 1948, pp. 128-136; Nathan Reich, chairman of economics dept. at Hunter College, "Jewish Life in the Russian Satellites," April, 1949, pp. 328-334; Solomon M. Schwarz, "The New Anti-Semitism of the Soviet Union," June, 1949, pp. 535-45.

The New Leader, N. Y.: Jacob Leschinsky [Lestchinsky] (of Yiddish Scientific Institute of Wilno), March 8, 1947 (alleges Russia's Jews were evacuated in front of Hitler's armies only insofar as economically valuable); Jacob Pat, exec. sec'y of the Jewish Labor Committee, "The Fate of the Jews in the Soviet Union," May 3, 1947, p. 8, & "Anti-Semitism in Soviet Russia," June 5, 1948, p. 9; David J. Dallin, March 6, 1948, p. 2 & Jan. 31, 1948, p. 1, col. 2, etc.; Jacob Leschinsky, "Soviet 'Jewish Homeland': The Real Facts about Biro-Bidjan," April 17, 1948, p. 4; Max Nomad, "Anti-Semitism in the USSR," June 12, 1948; Mark Alexander (Near East correspondent), "The Kremlin Turns On Israel," April 16, 1949, p. 4; Boris I. Nicolaevsky, "Moscow Awaits Changes," April 23, 1949, p. 11; Solomon Schwarz (of New School of Social Research), "Jingoism in the USSR: Anti-Semitic Innuendoes Spice Drive on 'Cosmopolitans,' " June 4, 1949, p. 8.

Politics, ed. by Dwight Macdonald, N. Y.; Melvin J. Lasky, "Interview with a Prisoner" (returned from several years in Russia), Spring, 1948; pp. 88-90; & other issues.

Newsweek, N. Y., diplomatic correspondent Edward Weintal; Dec. 29, 1947; April 4, 1949, pp. 11, 30; May 2, 1949, p. 35.

Plain Talk, N. Y.: Herschel Weinrauch, "Stalin Purges Jewish Writers," Feb., 1949, pp. 39-41; April, 1949, p. 53, letter by Weinrauch on "Fate of Russian Jews" (rebuts the skeptical review of his above article by Alfred Werner in *Congress Weekly,* Feb., 1949); Louis Jay Herman, "The Communist Record on Palestine," Jan., 1949, pp. 19-25; & other issues.

Harper's Magazine, N. Y.: Ben Horin, "Soviet Wooing of Palestine," April, 1944.

New Republic, N. Y.: J. L. Teller, director, Office of Jewish Information of the American Jewish Congress, "Israel & the Iron Curtain," April 11, 1949; pp. 16-17 (quotes Soviet sources on renewed anti-Zionist drive of 1949).

N. Y. Times: March 15, 1949; p. 17, "Russia Penalizes 2 Literary Critics." Dispatches by Prof. Harry Schwartz on Soviet anti-semitism: March 31, 1949, p. 11; April 8, p. 9, cols. 3-4; April 20, p. 15, col. 1; May 7, p. 3, col. 1; May 12, p. 6, cols. 3-4, preceded by U.P. dispatch from Moscow on same theme. May 1, 1949; p. 78, cols. 2-3 on purge of Jewish architects. May 2, 1949; p. 13, cols. 2 and 3; C. L. Sulzberger dispatch. May 20, p. 6, cols. 2-3, quotes Soviet attack on three Jewish economists as "cosmopolitan." May 24, dispatch of May 23 from Atlantic City, headlined "Anti-Jewish Acts By Soviets Scored;"

quotes the president of the Rabbinical Council of America concerning reports that "a systematic attempt is being carried on to suppress the religious, social, and cultural life of the Jewish people in Poland, Rumania, Hungary and other countries under Soviet domination." June 11, p. 5, middle of col. 3, headlined "Taunts Over Jewish Wife Impel Soviet Flyer to Flee."

Library of Jewish Information, American Jewish Committee, bulletin of March 8, 1949, "The New Campaign Against Zionism," quotes attacks from Soviet and satellite press against Jewish "double allegiance." Bulletin of April 1, "Jews Behind the Iron Curtain," includes a section headed: "The Campaign against 'Homeless Cosmopolitans' Hits Russian Jews," as well as sections on Jews in the satellite countries.

Sotsialistichiski Vyestnik, Russian-language socialist magazine, N. Y., April, 1949; S. Schwartz, "Nationalism and Anti-semitism in the Soviet Union," pp. 55-57; quotes, in original Russian, anti-semitic anti-cosmopolitan attacks from such Soviet primary sources as *Pravda, Literaturnaya Gazeta,* etc. Another article with similar quotations follows on p. 58.

Aufbau, German-language newspaper dedicated to Jewish problems, Friday, May 13, 1949; Michael Wurmbrand, "Moscow's Anti-Jewish Offensive," p. 9, describes "purges of Jewish intellectuals" and cites primary sources of current Soviet press. Also other issues, including article of April 8 headlined "Bad Times for Russia's Jews."

Jewish Daily Forward, N. Y., Jan. 8, 1938; article by G. Aronson, listing from Soviet press the preponderance of Jewish names among victims of the 1936-38 anti-Trotskyist purges; this earlier material may perhaps be relevant to the 1949 anti-semitism.

Contemporary Jewish Record, published bi-monthly by American Jewish Committee and now superseded, N. Y.: Alexander S. Kohanski, "Communist Propaganda for Jews," Sept.-Oct., 1940, vol. III, No. 5, pp. 470-483; Abraham Weiss, "In Nazi Warsaw," same issue, pp. 495-6 on Soviet rebuffing of Jewish refugees from Nazism; Jacob Lestchinsky (spelled "Leschinsky" in his later *New Leader* articles), "Jews in the U.S.S.R.," same issue, pp. 510-26, with 2nd instalment in Nov.-Dec. issue, 1940, vol. III, No. 6, pp. 607-621. At the Atlantic City Convention of the Jewish Labor Committee, Feb. 24-27, 1949, Dr. Emmanuel Pat read a long report on "Jews Behind The Iron Curtain," alleging discrimination. *Labor Action,* journal of a junior Trotskyist faction, April 11, 1949, cites examples of such persecution. Joseph Starobin in N. Y. *Daily Worker,* April 14, 15, 16, 1949, gives Communist rebuttal to charges of Soviet anti-semitism; also Robert Friedman, Friday, May 13, pp. 12-14, "How Times, Post, Newsweek Lied Against USSR On Anti-Semitism."

2. Edward Weintal in *Newsweek* magazine, N. Y., April 4, 1949; p. 30. Harry Schwartz, *N. Y. Times,* May 12, 1949; p. 6, cols. 3-4. According to Solomon Schwarz, who has likewise made a special survey of this problem from primary sources, the proportion of Jews among the attacked cosmopolitans is more than two-thirds; Solomon Schwarz, "Jingoism in the USSR: Anti-Semitic Innuendoes Spice Drive on 'Cosmopolitans'," in *New Leader,* June 4, 1949; p. 8.

3. Weintal, *loc. cit.* Added examples of Soviet exposures of Jewish last names cited in *N. Y. Times,* March 31, 1949, p. 11; May 2, p. 13,

Appendix / 189

cols. 2-3; May 7, p. 3, col. 1; May 20, p. 6, cols. 2-3; and in *Sotsialis-tichiski Vyestnik*, N. Y., April, 1949, pp. 55-58; etc.

4. Weintal, *loc. cit.*

5. *N. Y. Times*, March 31, 1949; p. 11; dispatch by Prof. Harry Schwartz, headlined "Communists Here To Fight Zionism." Russia's Jewish magazine *Der Shtern* has now been suspended, too.

6. J. L. Teller, director of the Office of Jewish Information of the American Jewish Congress, "Israel and the Iron Curtain," article in *The New Republic*, N. Y., April 11, 1949; p. 16.

7. Prof. Harry Schwartz, "Has Russia Solved The Jewish Problem?" article in *Commentary* magazine, N. Y., Feb., 1948; p. 130.

8. David J. Dallin, "Stalin & Molotov in 1939-41 & 1945-48," article in *The New Leader*, Jan. 31, 1948; p. 1, col. 2, paragraph 3. Abraham Weiss, "In Nazi Warsaw," in *Contemporary Jewish Record*, N. Y., vol. III, No. 5, Sept.-Oct., 1940, pp. 495-6.

9. Schwartz, *loc. cit.*, 130-3. Estimate in *American Jewish Year Book, 1947-1948*, is by G. J. Gliksman. Jerzy Gliksman, *Tell The West*, N. Y., Gresham Press, 1948 (by a Polish Jewish socialist who served in Soviet Russia as a slave laborer) gives detailed account of fate of both non-Jews and Jews in Soviet labor camps after the fall of Poland.

10. Schwartz, *loc. cit.*, 130-3. Kiev and other Ukrainian pogroms described in *Bulletin* of Joint Rescue Committee of Jewish Agency for Palestine, March, 1945, pp. 19, ff.; also later issues, April, 1945, May, 1946, August, 1947, etc.

11. In National Archives Building in Washington and partly published and discussed in *Der Monat*, ed. by Melvin J. Lasky, Berlin, Information Services Division, APO 742, Jahrgang I, Nummer 2, Nov., 1948 and subsequent issues. The issue of Nov., 1948 contains some extremely important and hitherto secret Seeckt material entitled "Der Seeckt-Plan," pp. 42-58, including: Julius Epstein, "Aus unveröffent-lichten Dokumenten," pp. 42-50; Eugen Fischer-Baling, "Politik und Kriegsromantik," pp. 50-55; M. J. Lasky, "Seeckt, Stalin und Europa," pp. 55-58. Less dramatic but also a valuable source on Soviet-Reichs-wehr collaboration are those posthumous papers of Colonel-General Hans von Seeckt (1866-1936) which were published in Germany during the pact under the title *Aus Seinem Leben*, Leipzig, Hase und Koehler, [1940].

12. Ruth Fischer, *Stalin and German Communism*, Cambridge, Harvard Univ. Press, 1948.

13. Melvin J. Lasky, "New Light on Moscow Trials: Did Hitler Help Stalin in the Frame-Up?" *The New Leader*, Dec. 25, 1948; pp. 8-9. Article on Soviet-German relations by Robert Ingram in *Schweizer Monathefte*, May, 1948. Two articles in *Foreign Affairs*, N. Y., Oct., 1946: DeWitt C. Poole, "Light on Nazi Foreign Policy" and John W. Wheeler-Bennett, "Twenty Years of Russo-German Relations, 1919-1939." U. S. State Dept. publication of *Nazi-Soviet Relations, 1939-41: Documents from the Archives of the German Foreign Office*, Washington, 1948, obtainable for $1 from the Superintendent of Documents, Washington, D. C.; these documents establish that Stalin, not Hitler, took the initiative in the alliance and suggest that Russia was the sincere, Germany the insincere member of the pact that Hitler violated in 1941. J. Alsop and R. Kintner, *American White Paper*, 7th ed., N. Y.,

1940, p. 52: Stalin initiated conversations with Hitler for an anti-western partnership of the twin totalitarians as early as 1934, with spasmodic diplomatic exchanges continuing until the apparent triumph of Stalin's wooing in the '39 pact.

George W. F. Hallgarten, "General Hans von Seeckt and Russia, 1920-1922," in *Journal of Modern History*, Chicago, March, 1949, pp. 28-34; analyzes important documents about Rapallo from the *Heeresarchiv* in Potsdam, now in the National Archives in Washington.

The following books provide a more general background on Soviet-German relations. David J. Dallin, *Soviet Russia's Foreign Policy, 1939-42*, New Haven, Yale Univ. Press, 1942 and *The Real Soviet Russia*, New Haven, Yale Univ. Press, 1944. Louis Fischer, *The Soviets in World Affairs*, published by Cape and Smith, 1930, 2 vols., covering 1917-29. Max Beloff, *The Foreign Policy of Soviet Russia*, Oxford Univ. Press, 1947; stresses Far East more than west. Franz Borkenau, *World Communism*, N. Y., Norton, 1939; history of 3d International. T. A. Taracouzio, *War and Peace in Soviet Diplomacy*, N. Y., Macmillan, 1940. W. G. Krivitsky, *In Stalin's Secret Service*, N. Y., Harper, 1939; an insider's version of the 1938 purges by former chief of Soviet military intelligence in western Europe; denounced by Communists as a traitor, Krivitsky was subsequently found shot in an American hotel room and presumed a suicide. S. W. Halperin, *Germany Tried Democracy; a Political History of the Reich from 1918 to 1933*, N. Y., Crowell Co. [1946]; describes how Nazis and Communists, attacking from right and left, wrecked German democracy. Prof. O. K. Flechtheim, *Die Kommunistische Partei Deutschlands in der Weimarer Republik*, Offenbach a.M., Bollwerk-Verlag K. Drott, 1948; primary sources about German communism.

Julius Epstein, "The Rechberg Affidavit, Stalin's Aid to Hitler," *The New Leader*, Aug. 7, 1948. Epstein accepts as valid this debatable affidavit, admitted as relevant by the American Military Tribunal at Nuremberg, April 28, 1948, during the I. G. Farben trials. While I would accept as valid the general picture of Soviet-Reichswehr relations presented in the well-documented Seeckt and Fischer material, following in this the judgment of such authorities as Prof. Sidney Fay, Prof. Hans Kohn, and most other historians of the period, yet I must urge suspended judgment on the insufficiently-documented Rechberg affidavit until it is either disproved or proved by the captured German documents in Washington, which are too numerous and unorganized to have as yet been assimilated by historians (except for such outstanding material as the Seeckt data). We already know that the Soviet government before 1933, while verbally anti-Nazi, was directing the attacks of German Communists mainly on the Social Democrats ("social fascists") and on the Weimar Republic and only secondarily on the Nazis. According to the Rechberg affidavit, Stalin in secret was even urging General Schleicher, political leader of the Reichswehr, to finance lavishly Hitler's successful campaign in the Reichstag elections of 1930, in order to re-establish the anti-western Soviet-German front of the Berlin treaty of 1926. Schleicher is quoted as saying:

"Stalin let me know that the situation was becoming more and more ripe for Russia and Germany [in 1930], since France and England neglected their armaments in their silly confidence in the League of Nations. But in order to achieve an active German-Russian policy, a rapid rearmament of Germany was necessary. I, General von Schleicher, had to start a campaign to that effect in Germany; and he, Stalin, believed that Hitler was the man suitable for that purpose. Therefore, the Reichswehr ought to finance Hitler."

14. *Der Monat*, ed. by M. J. Lasky, Berlin, Information Services Division, APO 742, Jahrgang I, Nummer 2, Nov. 1948; "Der Seeckt-Plan," pp. 42-58; and subsequent numbers.

15. Ruth Fischer, *Stalin and German Communism*, Cambridge, Harvard Univ. Press, 1948; for this quotation and similar material, see pp. 524-36, 655-57, 662-63.

16. Quoted from the full text of Viacheslav Molotov's report delivered on October 31 in Moscow to the Fifth Extraordinary Session of the Supreme Soviet of the USSR. *Soviet Russia Today*, Communist monthly, N. Y., Nov. 1939; "Molotov's Report to Supreme Soviet," pp. 5-8, 47-50.

17. *Nazi-Soviet Relations, 1939-1941* ("documents from the archives of the German Foreign Office as released by the Department of State"), ed. by R. J. Sontag and J. S. Beddie, N. Y., Didier, 1948; p. 75.

18. Published in N. Y. *Daily Worker*, Communist newspaper, Dec. 26, 1939; p. 1, col. 6.

19. N. Y. *Daily Worker*, Oct. 10, 1939, under signature of foreign editor, Harry Gannes, p. 6.

20. For documents about Nazi Soviet trade agreements, see *Nazi-Soviet Relations*, pp. 131-34, 318-19, 327, 332, 339-41, and *passim*.

21. *Ibid.*, 236.

22. *Ibid.*, 339-41, signed "Schnurre," Berlin, May 15, 1941.

23. Hitler's decision to attack Russia was apparently made right after the breakdown of the Nov. 1940 negotiations over Soviet claims to Dardanelles, Balkans, and Finland. Evidence of this is the date of Dec. 18, 1940 on Hitler's "Top Secret: Operation Barbarossa" document, outlining the plan of attack. This document, "double-crossing" the Russians, was found in the German Wehrmacht archives; *ibid.*, 260-64. Still other documents show that even much earlier in 1940, Hitler was seriously considering a future surprise attack on his Soviet ally.

24. Stephen Naft, "Questions for Communists," in *The New Leader*, March 20, 1948; p. 4, middle of col. 2.

25. *Nazi-Soviet Relations*, p. 167. Interview of July 13, 1940 between Molotov and the German ambassador Schulenburg, recorded by the latter in a telegram from Moscow, dated July 13. Italics mine.

26. *Ibid.*, 338.

27. *Ibid.*, 324. For Stalin's pro-German leanings, see also pp. 335-6. Stalin also declared (see William Z. Foster's column, N. Y. *Daily Worker*, Dec. 27, 1939, p. 6, col. 5): "It was not Germany who attacked France and England but France and England who attacked Germany, assuming responsibility for the present war." Many years earlier, Stalin had said in an interview (quoted by David J. Dallin in *The New Leader*, June 18, 1949, p. 2, col. 3): "If one is to speak about our sympathies for any nation or, to be more correct, for the majority of any nation, one would, of course, speak about our sympathies for the Germans. There can be no comparison between these sympathies and our feelings for the Americans."

28. *Nazi-Soviet Relations*, 217-47, account of the Hitler-Molotov talks in Berlin in Nov. 1940; pp. 207-17 describe the preceding nego-

tiations with Stalin and Molotov by which Germany arranged for Molotov's visit to Berlin.

29. *Ibid.*, 233-34.

30. *Ibid.*, 234.

31. Nazi objections to Soviet plans for Dardanelles, Balkans, and Finland will be found *ibid.*, 284 and 301-305 (Ribbentrop to Matsuoka); 322 (Hitler to Schulenburg); 348 (declaration of war); and *passim.* Soviet demands for the Straits and Balkan gains will be found *ibid.*, 217-59 (note esp. p. 258); 270-72; and *passim.*

32. *Ibid.*, 301, 305.

33. Rosa Kaganovich, Lazar Kaganovich's sister, is presumed by most authorities to be Stalin's third wife; nevertheless, the close censorship surrounding Stalin's private life prevents any absolute certainty about this.

34. Josef Goebbels, *The Goebbels Diaries*, ed. by Louis Lochner, N. Y., Doubleday, 1948; p. 492: "Stalin's ouster of these Jews." Schwartz, *loc. cit.*, 129, 134-5.

35. *Newsweek*, Dec. 29, 1947; the quotation is part of Edward Weintal's summary of the conditions complained about by the Committee.

36. Jacob Leschinsky, of the Yiddish Scientific Institute of Wilno, "Soviet 'Jewish Homeland': The Real Facts about Biro-Bidjan," article in *The New Leader*, April 17, 1948; p. 4.

37. Frederick C. Barghoorn, "Notes on Life and Travel in Russia," in *Yale Review*, New Haven, summer, 1948.

38. Cf. the accounts by Jewish refugees from Russia and by former Jewish Partisans included in the bibliography of footnote (1) of Appendix, in Schwartz, *loc. cit.*, & in various issues, from March, 1945 on, of the *Bulletin* of the Joint Rescue Committee of the Jewish Agency for Palestine.

39. Prof. H. S. Muller, the genetics authority and Nobel Prize winner, writes in his article "The Destruction of Science in the USSR," *Saturday Review of Literature*, N. Y., Dec. 4, 1948, p. 65: "One curious effect of the Lysenko doctrine has been on the Communist conception of the nature of man and of racial and class differences. . . . Those living under favorable conditions would produce progressively better germ cells and so become innately superior. [Footnote by Muller:] (The writer was told in 1936 that this was the 'official' doctrine of the Communist Party . . .) In a word, we should have innate master and subject races and classes, as the Nazis so blatantly insisted."

40. Boris I. Nicolaevsky, "Moscow Awaits Changes," *New Leader*, April 23, 1949; p. 11.

41. *N. Y. Times*, Sunday, May 1, 1949; (U. P. dispatch of April 30 from London, quoting the reaction of diplomats to the *Soviet Art* announcements); p. 78, cols. 2-3.

42. Harry Schwartz, article headlined "Israel Is U. S. Tool, Reds Here Assert," *N. Y. Times*, April 8, 1949; p. 9, cols. 3-4.

43. Stalin, *Collected Works*, Russian edition, Moscow, 1946; II, 50-1. Above English translation of this passage is by Bertram Wolfe. *Three Who Made A Revolution*, N. Y., Doubleday, 1948; p. 468. Italics mine.

44. Wolfe, *op. cit.*, pp. 468-69. Aleksinsky (in some books spelt "Alexinsky") "did eventually become a full-edged anti-semite."

45. Joseph Starobin, foreign editor, N. Y. *Daily Worker*, articles of April 14, 15, and 16, 1949; Robert Friedman, May 13, pp. 12-14.